NANO

TECHNOLOGY OF MIND OVER MATTER

Kabbalah Publishing is a registered DBA of
Kabbalah Centre International, Inc.

For further information:

The Kabbalah Centre
155 E. 48th St., New York, NY 10017
1062 S. Robertson Blvd., Los Angeles, CA 90035

1.800.Kabbalah
www.kabbalah.com

First Edition March 2008
Printed in USA
ISBN10: 1-57189-582-5
ISBN13: 978-1-57189-582-0

Design: HL Design (Hyun Min Lee) www.hldesignco.com

NANO

TECHNOLOGY OF MIND OVER MATTER

www.kabbalah.com™

KABBALIST RAV BERG

FOREWORD

In all the years that I have known my father, I have to admit I have never seen the Rav so excited by a subject as he is about nanotechnology.

The Rav's excitement, however, might be misleading to some people. It was not, in any way, based on the obvious 1 Percent physical technology and the promise that nanotechnologists are speaking about. The Rav, as usual, saw far beyond that. In nanotechnology, the Rav found the language, the concepts, and the direct parallels with which to convey the most important aspects of Kabbalah's own technology.

The kabbalists of history always had great respect for science in that scientific truths are a direct reflection of the spiritual truths that underlie all reality. They mirror the revelation of the kabbalistic secrets taking place in the physical world, within the realm of human consciousness. In other words, as the kabbalists uncover new, lofty metaphysical truths encrypted into the texts of the *Zohar*, science immediately unlocks truths concerning the physical laws that govern the natural world. As human consciousness rises on a spiritual level, discoveries in physics and medical science automatically follow suit.

Kabbalists always embraced the sciences. It is now time for the sciences to embrace Kabbalah so that two sides of one coin can become whole.

The Rav, astonishingly, has achieved just that with this book. Nanotechnology is offering us nothing less than an opportunity to regenerate the human body and achieve the ultimate goal of biological immortality. The way in which nanotechnologists describe the methodologies for achieving such a grand goal mirrors precisely the formulae and techniques spoken of in the *Zohar* some twenty centuries ago. What was lacking was the ability to draw these parallels in a fashion that would be both achievable and intelligible to the average layperson.

The Cost

In all of his personal excitement, the Rav knew all along that his lifetime of monumental effort toward reaching this historic moment would come at a cost. My father was prepared to pay that cost, as all great kabbalists of history have done. And he did.

When kabbalists reveal secrets that are deep, secrets that are handed over to a generation not yet deemed worthy to appreciate and accept them, the souls of the kabbalists leave this world, or they must suffer tremendous emotional, physical, and spiritual pain.

This book began in the conference room of the Los Angeles-based Kabbalah Centre in 2003. From the time the Rav started writing, our goal was to have this book published and in the hands of the world by winter of 2004. God had other plans.

After a few months of writing with such passion and vigor, the Rav suddenly had a stroke. I knew immediately it was because of the secrets that the Rav was putting to paper. You see, a kabbalist is not a disseminator of information. Anyone can pass along information. A kabbalist must become a channel. Most people have no conception of what being a true channel means. The kabbalist, in order to channel, must become a living, breathing, shining example of the secrets that he wishes to convey to others. The kabbalist must embody all that he shares. In other words, it's not: *do as I say* but rather *do as I do and you too will achieve what I've achieved.*

The Rav has always been about one thing and one thing only: **mind over matter**. Kabbalistic nanotechnology is all about mind over matter. Consequently, before the Rav could transfer the wisdom of Kabbalah to paper, he had to live this concept so that others would have a well-trodden path that they could walk in order to achieve the same without having to suffer.

On September 2, 2004, the Rav was rushed to the hospital. Doctors said the Rav had a stroke. The neurosurgeon took my mother aside and told her that my father would be a vegetable because of the particular part of the brain that was afflicted and the large amount of damage sustained. It was Friday afternoon. Shabbat was nearly upon us. A few close friends rushed to the hospital to be with our family so that we could have at least 10 people for the Shabbat.

I knew deep in my soul, right then and there, that the Rav was not a victim of circumstance. Strokes are not random occurrences. No disease is. This was the Rav's conviction all his life. The Rav took on this fight, willingly, to put into practice what the ancient *Zohar* promised so long ago—that we, mankind, have the ability to achieve mind over matter and heal ourselves of all sickness and disease at the most fundamental level of reality, including our atoms, the subatomic particles that produce an atom, and far beyond that.

Shabbat Night

As the Rav lay motionless in the hospital room, with our close friends surrounding us, we entered into the Shabbat with a sense of total certainty of the Rav's recovery. Yet, I felt a deep, indescribable sense of pain at seeing such a powerful, loving, larger-than-life hero look so helpless, at least from the limited perspective of my own eyes. We opened the Rav's eyelids as he lay there in a comatose state. No one was home. It was a frightening image but yet, I still sensed a warm glow radiating from my father's face that filled me with certainty.

My beloved mother has the courage and compassion of the greatest of biblical heroines and matriarchs. And she has the soul and kindness of an angel. She knows my father better than anyone on Earth. My mother refused to accept what the neurosurgeon had told her. Not out of a sense of denial. Rather, it was her sense of knowing exactly who was lying in that hospital bed. My mother cried painful tears that night, yet she ran around that hospital room making sure all of our friends were comfortable and taken care of. She sat for hours in the lavatory, looking through its open door at the rest of the room, so that our friends could sit comfortably on chairs close around the Rav's bed. My heart was broken. Yet I knew I was seeing greatness beyond what words can describe. My mother, even in her greatest time of need, put the needs of others first.

As the late Friday sun began to descend into the western horizon and the awesome energy of Shabbat began to permeate the room, we started to sing *Lecha Dodi*, the famous hymn that has the power to attract and capture the incoming energy that the kabbalists call the *Shabbat Queen*, which is the female aspect of the Divine Force.

It was the hardest *Lecha Dodi* I had ever sung in my life. To feel total certainty in the teachings of Kabbalah, to have complete conviction in the power and greatness of my own father, and simultaneously to be experiencing the inconsolable pain that softens one's heart and wounds one's soul is quite a paradoxical and conflicted state of mind to find oneself in.

As the song began, I watched my dear brother Michael burst into tears uncontrollably, my mother too. I sobbed so hard I could not get the words of the song out. And then suddenly, in the middle of this ancient haunting melody, something shifted. The mood in the room was suddenly and inexplicably elevated. A spring of hope flowed through my heart.

The doctors were still adamant that my father would be a vegetable. They checked the charts. Brain damage is brain damage.

Many long hours into that night, around three in the morning, the Rav started moving his right hand. He was trying to glide it over his body, a healing technique that he used every day and taught to students all around the world. Then the Rav's mouth started moving. He was whispering, mumbling, but could not get any words out. And then, all of a sudden, the Rav started reciting a prayer. A minute later, all of us were singing *Lecha Dodi*. It was five long hours after we had originally sung it, but that's the Rav. He does things on his own schedule; he has his own timetable and he loves to take his time with everything that he does.

Needless to say, electricity filled the room. We opened the Rav's eyelids but still no one was there. My father was still unconscious. Yet he sang every word of the song. Such is the path of the kabbalist.

All of us in the room remained convinced that the Rav would make a miracle occur and he would do so before Shabbat ended at sundown Saturday night. All through the rest of the night and all day Saturday, the Rav was still unconscious. The doctors were still adamant that my mother would have to make a decision about life support because of the extensive brain damage.

The Third Meal

The Rav's favorite part of Shabbat has always been the Third Meal, which takes place late Saturday afternoon. According to the kabbalists, the Third Meal of Shabbat is a powerful and profound time of healing, especially to draw the power to fortify the immune system of the body and the immune system of the world. Third Meal energy is also all about the Final Redemption of mankind, a time when mind over matter will become the new reality.

It was during the Third Meal that the Rav did something quite spectacular. My father opened up his eyes and spoke coherently. The Rav then did the blessing over the wine, his eyes wide open, reciting each word. When he concluded, he drifted off to wherever it is he goes, and he fell back into his comatose state. But we all knew that the Rav was now in full control. It was mind over matter.

One of the doctors on staff, a cardiologist who was monitoring the Rav's heart, took aside one of our students, who also happened to be a cardiologist, and expressed utter amazement about the Rav. He demanded to know who that man was lying in that bed and pleaded with our friend to send him information about him.

During the Kabbalah Centre's Passover Event in Miami, Florida a few months later, one of the top neurosurgeons in the country, a doctor from Houston, Texas who had helped care for the Rav, stood up in front of two-thousand people. He said it was absolutely impossible for the Rav to be doing what he is doing, based upon the current damage in the Rav's brain. You see, before this neurosurgeon addressed the crowd, the Rav, physically strong and robust, had given a terrific lecture to the crowd. The neurosurgeon was clear: no medical journal on Earth could explain or account for the Rav's condition. It defied all the conventional wisdom of medical science.

Always Present

It is now four years later. The Rav is still not the Rav we knew. But neither are we the same people. The Rav took it upon himself to fight the root of chaos, the root of disease, and the root of the Angel of Death himself in a realm far more authentic than our physical world.

When I or others need the Rav physically, the old Rav shows up in an instant and it takes your breath away. He stays as long as one needs him and then a moment later the Rav is somewhere else fighting the good fight so that the rest of the world can soon be free of chaos and destruction. This is the battle all kabbalists fight, whether the world is aware of it or not.

What makes this particular battle unique and distinct from all others fought by kabbalists throughout history is that the Rav should not be here. Plain and simple. Yet he is. And the secrets that the Rav was revealing and writing about at the time of the stroke were the secrets of mind over matter, nanotechnology, and the methodology for achieving spiritual and biological immortality. Yes, kabbalists are big thinkers and they set lofty goals, regardless of what others may think. But the Rav never expects anyone to do anything that he has not done himself. The Rav never expects anyone to achieve anything that the Rav has not achieved himself. You see, the Rav cannot do it for us. No kabbalist can. It is the duty, birthright, and destiny of every person to achieve his or her own state of pure happiness, never-ending fulfillment, and everlasting life. That is the gift God gave each human being and, as you will read in the pages ahead, that is our destiny. The kabbalists do have the ability to share the secret with the world, but they only share secrets that they themselves live and embody.

The True Kabbalist

Two things determine whether one is a true kabbalist. First, he must have a bona fide, recognized teacher who is a master of Kabbalah, one who is responsible for transmitting the secret lore to his student. Second, he must live the principles that he will teach. My father buried a child so that he could share the solution and wisdom for alleviating grief in one's life. My father lost all of his money, leaving him and my mother financially destitute for years, so that he could teach the importance of appreciating a single penny. He was forced to sleep in his car and share a room with twenty strangers every night as he started out trying to build The Kabbalah Centre after the death of his teacher so that he could learn the power of sacrifice. He knocked on countless doors selling *Zohars* to learn the value of changing a single person's life in a single moment at their door-step. My father endured slander, persecution, and libel by the religious establishment so that he could discover the importance of spirituality over religiosity. He was humiliated, maligned, and vilified so that his ego would be ripped from his being in order that he may teach the purpose and value of authentic humility and true love of one's own soul. He watched his closest students, in whom he had invested twenty years of his life, loving and teaching them, turn on him and walk away to start teaching their own version of Kabbalah. This happened so that he could learn the importance of unconditional love, expecting nothing in return for the love that one gives. And after all this, when The Kabbalah Centre was booming with hundreds of teachers and thousands of students in Israel in the mid-1980s, my father watched the entire organization walk away over night, losing everything he had built. This lesson was to teach him persistence and constant trust in the Creator.

I cannot possibly include all the strange illnesses and debilitating pain that I watched him endure over the years. Through it all he smiled, and never complained. The defamation of his character never stopped, even to this very day. And I watched, first-hand, how it only made him stronger, more determined, and happier in the work that he was doing. I believe he learned that lesson for me.

My father literally slept two hours a night, every night of the week, for at least twenty years so that he would master the lesson of never yielding to the will of the body. I watched him pray hours upon hours, through the day, and then again rising every single night to pray through the night.

As The Kabbalah Centre re-expanded all over the world, he was forced to stay up twenty-two hours a day, in between his prayers, listening and helping to solve the heart-wrenching problems of people he loved all over the world. Their pain was his pain, as if his pain were not enough.

And so, in our quiet moments together, when the pressures seemed to be unbearable, my father often said to me in a moment of vulnerability. "People think I am made of iron. I am not." And I would reply, "That is why you are made of iron."

Therein lies the power of all the kabbalists of history and the greatness and Divinely-inspired determination of my loving father.

Many sections of this book were written by the Rav prior to his stroke in the fall of 2004. A lot of this book was written after it. Thus, you may notice a different tone or style at various times, but this is merely a reflection of the Rav's different states of consciousness. Naturally, the style and tone are not what's really important. The message is what's important.

In truth, the content of this book started being written many centuries ago. But the world was not yet ready, so the book, which is nothing less than the mysteries of the *Zohar* made easy, was never published. We missed our winter 2004 deadline, perhaps because our generation was also not yet ready to hear these startling truths and astonishing secrets. Well, something has changed. I am therefore jubilant beyond what words can describe because this book, this new and definitive understanding of the *Zohar* is now in your hands.

The fact that people from all walks of life are now privy to the wisdom and power inside this text means we have arrived at the time of our Final Redemption and the end of all chaos.

There is not a kabbalist in human history—from Rav Akiva, Rav Shimon bar Yohai, Rashi, Rav Abraham ben David of Posquieres, Nachmanides, all the way to Rav Isaac Luria (the Ari) and Rav Moses Haim Luzzatto (the Ramchal)—who was chosen to divulge scientific, kabbalistic secrets with such simplicity and elegance as the Rav has displayed in this book.

But, without question, it is upon the shoulders of the above mentioned kabbalists that the Rav stands. They all form one chain. The long lineage of kabbalists are merely different branches of one tree—the *Tree of Life*—emanating from a single root and seed known as Rav Shimon bar Yohai.

But I am nonetheless proud and privileged to know that it was my father, the Rav, who was chosen to deliver and make manifest this, the final message and blueprint for achieving what is the Holy Grail of science and ultimate dream of mankind—***immortality and the end of all death.***

Teachers and students around the world who really know the Rav, people who would take a bullet for my father, are *not* surprised that it's the Rav who is accomplishing all this.

Naturally, if you read the stories and biographies of the great kabbalists of history, all of their close students revered their particular master and considered him to be the greatest in all of history. This reverence in no way diminished the accomplishments and greatness of the previous kabbalists; it's just that each student feels a special bond to his or her teacher.

But there are two things different in our generation, and the Rav's close students know it. First, the Rav has my mother, Karen. My mom is a teacher and leader in her own right, an equal partner to the Rav. But she is also mother to an entire generation who, like Rachel, sheds tears for the pain of all people all over our world. Second, the Rav has produced this book, his greatest of all works, one that needs to be constantly re-read to unravel its endless depth of wisdom. I know this book is actually a sacred section of the Holy *Zohar* itself. Never has such clarity of thought, as it relates to an actual formula for immortality, been put to paper.

On behalf of my brother Michael and myself, I pray that everyone is touched by the shining splendor of the Rav's soul, the sharing consciousness that permeates every page, and the conviction and superhuman certainty that radiates from my father's being.

YEHUDA BERG

TABLE OF
CONTENTS

1		Introduction
11	Part One	**The Promise of Nano**
27	Part Two	**The Origins of Atom and Adam**
57	Part Three	**The Structure of Everything**
83	Part Four	**Greed and the Law of Attraction**
105	Part Five	**Consciousness and the Cause of Death**
115	Part Six	**The Heart and Science of Nanotechnology**
153	Part Seven	**The Heart of the Matter**
175	Part Eight	**The Path to the Once Unthinkable!**
207	Part Nine	**Enter the Robots**
217	Part Ten	**Speak to the Atom**
233	Part Eleven	**The Bombshell! (A Paradox Resolved)**
269		Epilogue

*"And speak to the rock before their eyes;
and it shall give forth its water."*

—NUMBERS 20:8

*"Moses raised his hand and struck the rock with
his staff twice, when an abundance of water
gushed forth, and the congregation and their
livestock drank."*

—NUMBERS 20:11

*"And he received the gold from their hand,
and he fashioned it, with an engraving tool,
and made a molten calf."*

—EXODUS 32:4

INTRODUCTION

THE POWER

Some of you will read this book and you will realize—with breath-taking clarity—the stunning and historic power of the teachings it contains. Some of you will not. Some of you will recognize the profound implications of the technology presented in the following pages. Some of you will not. For many, this book will unleash a transformation so profound it will alter your reality in ways you might not dare dream or imagine. For others, this book may very well seem insignificant and far-fetched.

This is not unusual, nor is it unexpected, for this is how it has always been when kabbalistic wisdom is revealed. There is an old adage: *When the student is ready, the teacher will appear.*

MEETING THE MASTER

When I first met my teacher, the renowned Kabbalist Rav Yehuda Brandwein, in Jerusalem, I felt as though I was meeting a man transported straight out of the Middle Ages, although the year was 1962. His appearance, his demeanor, and his speech were obviously from another time. It was my first-ever encounter with anyone who had extensively explored the mysteries of Kabbalah. Although I myself had a background in divinity, having obtained rabbinical ordination as well as pursuing post-graduate rabbinical studies, Kabbalah had been a prohibited area of study.

The prohibition didn't bother me personally, for I had zero interest in the subject. As far as I was concerned, I had a greater chance of flying to the moon than of entering into the inner sanctums of kabbalistic wisdom. Yet here I was, about to meet a genuine kabbalist for the first time in my life. I had no idea what to expect. I wasn't sure what we could talk about. I knew beforehand that he had never attended a major university. In fact, he had probably never even heard of Harvard. He had never received any formal secular education. He had never studied the sciences. His only education was in the Torah and in Kabbalah.

My only option was to talk about the Bible. And so we did. I remember being utterly surprised by Rav Brandwein's comprehensive knowledge and his insights into biblical matters. He asked me if I knew anything about Kabbalah or the great kabbalists who lived throughout the ages. I told him I did not. The only kabbalist I had heard of was Rav Shimon, the son of Yohai, who lived approximately 2000 years ago and was the author of the *Zohar*, the most important book of Kabbalah. That was the full extent of my knowledge.

Two Worlds Collide

Some years earlier, when traditional organized religion failed to answer to my satisfaction the really challenging questions that all rabbis and priests confront at one time or another, I left it. I went into the insurance business, insuring municipalities and boroughs in New York City. I became involved in real estate development, New York City politics, and philanthropy. I had the honor of being served the first-ever kosher meal at the White House during the Kennedy Administration. So it is not an exaggeration to say that when I first met my teacher, I saw it as the collision of two totally opposed worlds—a businessman from the modern-day western world who had left the religious establishment in search of material wealth, and a kabbalist seemingly lifted right out of ancient Jerusalem who sought spiritual treasures. I was intensely curious about this man for a number of reasons, none of which had anything to do with Kabbalah.

Rav Brandwein was an ultra-orthodox kabbalist who lived according to a strict code of law, yet he was also the Chief Rabbi of the powerful Labor Union in Israel. For those of you not familiar with the culture of Israel, you should know that the Labor Union despised religion. They were the ultimate anti-religious group in the middle of the Holy Land, which is why I found their choice of Rav Brandwein so perplexing. Why had this religion-hating Labor Union chosen an ultra-orthodox kabbalist as their Chief Rabbi? The paradox fascinated me.

I had spent a lot of time in Israel. Without question, this was a country where the lines of demarcation were abundantly clear when it came to the Orthodox community—you were either in or you were out!

If you were a member of the right-wing orthodox community, you had zero tolerance for anything or anyone that represented Conservative or Reform Judaism, or, heaven forbid, the secular world. Likewise, if you were a reform Jew there was an unmistakable line between you and conservative Jews.

Yet here were two extreme opposites—one million members of an anti-religious labor union and one ultra-orthodox kabbalist— who had chosen to build their futures together. Even their style of dress was dramatically different. My future teacher wore garments that gave him the appearance of a deeply religious individual, one who might have lived a thousand years ago. The labor union people wore casual modern clothing. On every level, this was a marriage between two cultures at extreme opposite ends of the spectrum. I had never seen such a bizarre relationship before. And I knew it did not exist anywhere else in this world.

The Fusing of Opposites

This anomaly, this merging of two opposites, lies at the heart of all kabbalistic teachings. It is also the key to achieving nanotechnology—the control of matter on the molecular level. Little did I realize that this dichotomy would lead me to search for and find the ultimate reality that is the subject of this book.

In the years that followed, I watched the relationship between my teacher and members of the Labor Union blossom in the most profound way. Simple laborers, many of whom were uneducated and illiterate, loved and revered my teacher with a devotion I had never seen or experienced before. Rav Brandwein was as far from their world as east is from west. Yet they embraced him with a love and appreciation I never knew could exist between similarly-minded people, much less the anti-religious and the ultra-orthodox, whose relationship in Israel was so poisoned by hatred.

It became obvious to me that this man possessed some magical influence that enabled him to create the conditions for two opposite worlds to meet on common ground. This was not just tolerance, or a peace treaty between warring factions, which in itself would be commendable in a place like Israel. Here there was an abundance of love, a reverence that flowed between the two sides. What I saw with my teacher and the people of the Labor Union was love that transcended self-interest and personal need; a love that had no agenda, no self-consideration. This was just pure emotion, flowing unconditionally.

The Differences between Love and Need

When you ask someone why he or she loves another person, nine times out of ten they will tell you how wonderful that other person makes them feel. They will tell you that the other person makes them feel secure and loved; the other person treats them with respect and kindness. The other person is loyal to them.

According to Kabbalah that is not true love. The person is telling you all about what they are receiving—*not what they are giving.* Love means giving of yourself completely, sharing unconditionally without any concern for what you are receiving from the relationship. It's not about how the *other person* makes you feel but rather, it's about how you make the *other* person feel. Your care, concern, and love for the other person are unconditional. It is unqualified. There are no strings attached. There is not a trace of self-interest. With genuine love, the act of loving itself is the source of our pleasure.

The vast majority of marriages, relationships, and partnerships are based upon need, not love. I learned this profound lesson from my teacher and the relationships that he had built in his life.

An Arab and a Jew

I remember one particular incident that took place in 1967, while Rav Brandwein and I were studying together. First of all, you should know that in 1948, East Jerusalem was Arab territory. That changed after the Six-Day War in 1967, when Jerusalem became part of Israel. However, between 1948 and 1967, Arabs were not allowed to travel to the city of Tel Aviv.

Shortly after the Six-Day War had ended, an Arab peasant traveled all the way from Jerusalem to Tel Aviv with a small basket of grapefruits for my teacher. As I was standing there, this gentle Arab peasant told Rav Brandwein that he had waited since 1947 to bring him this gift. He had dreamed of this day for twenty long years. As soon as the war had ended, he immediately made the journey to visit my teacher. I was flabbergasted to say the least. *Why would an Arab peasant spend twenty years dreaming of seeing my teacher and bringing him a basket of fruit?*

It turned out that my teacher had offered aid and friendship to this man many years past, when he was in need of some help. Back then it was unthinkable for a Jew to help out an Arab. But my teacher only saw the soul of a person, not his or her religion or nationality.

On the surface, this was just a simple act of kindness on the part of my teacher. Simple acts of kindness between people happen all the time. Furthermore, their friendship was brief. So this gesture alone could not explain why this Arab was experiencing such intense warm feelings for Rav Brandwein, which was all the more peculiar given the extreme animosity that had divided Arabs and

Jews during those long years of violent hostility. What, then, was different about this situation? What I witnessed was not just a nice friendship. When I saw the way this man looked at my teacher and the joy that he experienced when presenting him with the grapefruit, I knew I saw a kind of love that I had never seen before. And then I learned why.

My teacher gave this man unconditional friendship, and he wanted nothing in return. Nothing. My teacher looked into this man's soul and offered him love for no reason. *He loved him for no reason at all.* It was not the aid that had touched this Arab. It was the love. When a person gives love *without an inkling of self-interest,* it penetrates to the core of another individual, beyond what we can imagine. It might happen in a brief encounter, yet it will last for eternity.

Once again I stood witness as all the space that could potentially separate one man from another was totally removed.

Space?

Yes, space. It is space that creates separation between people and cultures. Space is the problem. I didn't know it then, but I had just discovered the key to Kabbalah-Nanotechnology, and the ultimate dream of humanity: IMMORTALITY.

PART ONE:

THE
PROMISE
OF NANO

SO MUCH, SO FAST!

Two emerging technologies promise to transform our present day world in ways that make the breakthroughs of the 20th century pale in comparison. One is called nanotechnology. The other is called Kabbalah. One is less than 50 years old. The other has been around for some 4000 years. On the surface, they appear to be divergent, even contradictory disciplines. But in truth, they are astonishingly complementary.

IS THIS FOR REAL?

At first glance one might ask the obvious question: Kabbalah and nanotechnology—science and religion—isn't that an obvious mismatch? And how could Kabbalah possibly be a technology when it is supposed to be a sacred aspect of religion? These are valid questions, indeed. First of all, we must do one thing which most of us will find difficult: *leave religion out of this.* Kabbalah has nothing at all to do with religion. According to the ancient sages of Kabbalah, God never imposed organized religion upon mankind. Religion is a man-made invention. Religion is a corruption of the power that the Light Force of *God* gave humanity 3400 years ago on Mount Sinai. Kabbalah is not a religion any more than quantum physics or Einstein's theory of relativity is a religion.

OLD HABITS DIE HARD

The underlying point should be evident: religiosity is a narrow view provided by a particular belief—or non-belief—system.

UNIVERSAL PRINCIPLES

Kabbalah is universal, meaning that it reveals the Universal Laws that operate in both the seen *and* the unseen levels of our reality. Kabbalah embraces all the sciences and all true spiritual doctrines. It embraces opposite viewpoints and positions and does not claim to be the only truth. Kabbalah is a methodology for identifying and uniting all disciplines, all teachings, and all beliefs in order to reveal the underlying truth. Kabbalah's sole purpose is to fulfill our basic human desire to be deeply contented and absolutely fulfilled.

What, then, do Kabbalah and nanotechnology have in common?

THE
KABBALAH-NANO
CONNECTION

Kabbalah is all about attaining control over the physical world, including our personal lives, at the most fundamental level of reality. It's about achieving and extending mind over matter and developing the ability to create fulfillment, joy, and happiness by controlling everything at the most basic level of existence.

Nanotechnology offers a similar promise. In a report presented to the U.S. House of Representatives Committee on Science, at the turn of the century, the ultimate goal of nanotechnology was stated quite clearly:

> **Complete control of the physical structure of matter, all the way down to the atomic level.**
> —*Molecular Manufacturing: Societal Implications of Advanced Nanotechnology by: Christine Peterson, KunzweilAI.net*

Through nanotechnology we can get down to the level where we can manipulate the world of atoms and molecules in order to provide the world with unlimited energy, an endless supply of food, and the end of disease. In order to understand the promise and power of nanotechnology from the perspective of the ancient science of Kabbalah, first we need to understand a bit more about this fascinating new technology from the perspective of contemporary science.

WHAT IS "NANO?"

The word *nano* refers to a nanometer. A nanometer is a unit of measure equal to a billionth of a meter. If math is not one of your strengths, consider the almost unimaginable smallness of an atom, the building blocks of the Universe. If you lined up 100 million atoms in a row it would be as long as the line below:

—

A single drop of water contains one hundred billion, billion atoms. Nanotechnology is about downsizing and building things on that tiny scale.

A Cosmic Alphabet

All the words of the English language derive from the same 26-letter alphabet. This limited number of letters can be rearranged to create countless words with totally different meanings. Imagine an endless supply of letters from the alphabet floating all around you. You could pluck letters out of the air at any time to form any conceivable word in the English language. You could grab the letters *E—I—V—C—L—H—E* and create the word *vehicle*. You could take hold of the letters *L—E—P—A—P* and create the word *apple*.

Atoms work the same way. Atoms are the *alphabet* of our physical world, arranged to create all kinds of matter. Atoms configured one way create the air that we breathe. Atoms arranged differently create toxic waste. Those same atoms rearranged yet another way create the flowers we love. *Everything* we see—from stars in the heavens to sand pebbles on the beach—is made from the same "atomic alphabet."

If we could actually grab hold of atoms, we could, in theory, create anything we want. But there is a problem: *space!* We live in a large-scale world in which we cannot even see atoms, let alone touch them. If we cannot see them or touch them, how then can we manipulate them?

Enter the robots.

NANO ROBOTS

To solve this problem of space, scientists envision the creation of nano robots to help fulfill the promise of nanotechnology. These tiny robots would be the same size as atoms. Nano robots would be programmed to construct products atom by atom, molecule by molecule. Imagine the possibilities! Nano robots could take ordinary garbage and break it all down into its raw atoms. Using these same *disassembled* atoms as raw material, the robots could now be programmed to build new products such as clothes, food, or exercise machines. It would be like taking an airplane made out of Legos, disassembling it, and then using those same blocks to build a house.

The End of Garbage

Nano robots could help this planet achieve the ultimate in recycling, bringing about an end to environmental degradation and pollution. For instance, today we have large factories manufacturing consumer goods from various raw materials. But during the manufacturing process all kinds of wastes, including toxic wastes, are discharged into the environment. Nano-sized factories or robots could produce the same products from raw atoms *without* any waste by-products. What's more, those raw atoms (the building blocks) could come from dirt, cut grass, yesterday's newspaper, or any form of trash from your local waste management company. Pre-existing toxic waste could be rendered harmless simply by sending in nano robots to rearrange the atoms of the toxic waste into a new and safe configuration.

Resurrection of the Dead (Tissue)

Scientists foresee astonishing developments in the field of nano-medicine. Damaged hearts will be rebuilt atom-by-atom simply by sending a swarm of nano robots into the body. Body parts that have aged and deteriorated will be rebuilt from scratch, molecule by molecule.

Superhuman

There is a lot of empty space in our bones. Some nanotechnologists tell us that if we could inject pure diamond fibers into that empty space, bone strength would surpass steel. Through nanotechnology the rest of our bodies also could be infused with diamond fabric. Scientists have already calculated that this kind of diamond-based *body reinforcement* would have "G" force tolerance. In other words, one could fall off a building and walk away unscathed.

Nano-Immunity

Hundreds of tiny nano robots with the brainpower of a mainframe computer could be inserted into the space of a human cell. They could patrol the body like an artificial immune system, destroying anything foreign to the cell's DNA, including HIV, smallpox, SARS, Ebola, or any other exotic virus. Bio-terrorism would cease to be a threat.

Let's take a look at a few other ideas circulating in the field of nanotechnology.

Clouds of Glory

Scientists at Rutgers University are researching the development of a "utility fog." This fog is not made up of trillions of water droplets like a typical London fog. Utility fog is made up of air carrying trillions of germ-sized nano robots called "foglets." Each one of these trillions of molecular-sized robots would have the micro-processing power of a mainframe computer. This fog could fill part of a room in your home and be practically invisible. These trillions of tiny robots would be able to assemble atoms and molecules to create new furniture, food, or a large-screen plasma TV. The fog could descend upon a remote famine-stricken village and transform it into a paradise, creating beautiful houses, furniture, and an endless supply of food, simply by manipulating the limitless atoms in our midst. The fog could weave through a hurricane-stricken town repairing damaged homes, businesses, trees, and streets quickly and inexpensively.

A "Maytag" Nano Factory

A compact nano factory, the size of a washing machine, could be equipped with millions of tiny nano robots that disassemble the molecules of a particular chemical poured into the machine and reassemble those same molecules into a different product. According to nanotechnologists, if you poured $20 worth of raw chemicals into the nano factory, you could reassemble all those molecules into 200 cell phones, or 100 pairs of shoes. You could even build *another* compact nano factory. Villages in poverty-stricken regions could each have their own compact nano factory supplying them with food, clothes, furniture, and other necessities of life for just a few dollars. Famine and poverty could be eradicated from the landscape of civilization.

What if we run out of atoms and molecules to create new food and new housing? First, as I mentioned, we can use the atoms from our waste products. Second, and more exciting, there is a nearly endless supply of molecules right in front of our noses.

THE SECRET OF THE ATOM

The Extraordinary Trait of a Single Atom

Atoms have one distinct feature. This unique quality lies at the heart of kabbalistic teachings concerning the concept of immortality and control over the physical world. This feature relates directly to what I consider to be one of the greatest secrets in the entire body of kabbalistic wisdom. Let us take a closer look at this special quality and discover its practical benefits.

Science tells us that atoms are immortal, and the great kabbalists in history wholeheartedly agree with that observation. Atoms don't wear out like our clothes or the tires on our cars. This leads to a haunting question: If our atoms do not wear out, why then do we age? Why do furniture, carpets, and our favorite pair of shoes undergo wear and tear? Why do cars rust if the atoms that form the cars never become worn? Once again, these are very important questions from the perspective of Kabbalah.

It's About the Bond

Atoms group together by creating bonds with one another. In simpler terms, atoms "*hold hands.*" When two or more atoms connect, they form a molecule. Molecules are the building blocks of all physical matter, from alligators to zucchini.

ATOMS BONDED TOGETHER CREATE A MOLECULE.

When the Bond Breaks

When atoms stop holding hands, molecules break apart. They begin to vanish, which from our perspective appears as wear and tear, or deterioration.

**BONDS BETWEEN ATOMS BREAK, CREATING INDIVIDUAL ATOMS.
THE MOLECULE NO LONGER EXISTS.**

But the individual atoms live on. In fact, when a person dies, his or her atoms are as brand spanking new as they were the day that person was born. The person's atoms simply circulate back into the environment.

This means that the atoms that constituted the body of Abraham Lincoln are still among us. Atoms from the bodies of Napoleon, Alexander the Great, Shakespeare, Isaac Newton, Jesus, and Moses are still circulating in our midst. In fact, science says that in all probability, billions of atoms inside of you right now were once part of Mozart or Joan of Arc or the prophet Muhammad, or Buddha, or a star that shone in deep space a hundred million years ago.

So, when the fabric on your couch fades or when the carpet frays, remember that the atoms themselves remain as new and as fresh as they were billions of years ago. If you break something by accident, or if a living creature ages and dies, the atoms that constituted the object or person did not break or wear out. Physicists tell us it is only the *bond* between the groups of atoms that has splintered.

THE PROMISE
OF NANO

Through nanotechnology, atoms can be joined together much more effectively. We can, in theory, build products atom by atom, creating material with extraordinary bond strength that will prevent these products from ever wearing out. And if atoms do not let go of one another, molecules will not die. Nanotechnologists promise us a tennis ball that would never stop bouncing, shoes that never wear out, clothes that would never tatter, and human bodies that could constantly regenerate.

And if for whatever reason atomic bonds do break apart, nano robots could be there to repair the damage, plucking new atoms out of the air and using them to fix whatever broke. Nano robots could perform delicate surgery on an atomic level thousands of times more precisely than the most skillful surgeon wielding a scalpel. With no scars! They could regenerate damaged livers or disassemble dangerous tumors atom by atom. Airborne nano robots could rebuild a damaged ozone layer or transform nuclear waste into harmless new elements.

In Summary

Nanotechnology refers to manufacturing at the scale of atoms and molecules. Nano robots manipulate the atoms. Utilizing these raw atoms, nano robots can create anything, including new body parts, ozone layers, and household appliances. Atoms are immortal. They never wear out. Only the bonds between atoms break, causing the "death" of the molecule, which, in turn, manifests as wear and tear, aging, and decay.

Kabbalists have never been intrigued by the "how" of things, but have rather been trained to ask the question "why?" Why was the physical world created? Why did the Big Bang occur in the first place? What existed before there was even a Universe? What caused the atom to come into existence? Perhaps the most important practical question relating to nanotechnology is what causes atoms to stop holding hands? Once we know, will we have found a way to overcome death and create a world of peace and unending fulfillment?

My friends, there are no more important questions than these. Once the world knows the answers, the meaning of our lives will be revealed. Beyond that, a technology for creating nothing less than a world of peace and immortality will be within the grasp of humanity. So let's now travel back and discover what was before the Universe even existed.

PART TWO:

THE ORIGINS
OF ATOM
AND ADAM

HOW IT ALL BEGAN

A physicist is the atoms' way of thinking about atoms.
—Anonymous

The subject of Creation has been dealt with at great length in many of the books I have written. I will, therefore, present a brief, condensed account here to provide context for the topic of nanotechnology. A second and more important reason for presenting the process of Creation in simple fashion relates directly to a lesson taught to me by my teacher. Rav Brandwein said if something is overly complex and difficult to grasp, chances are it's not true. Truth is always simple enough for even a small child to understand.

According to the ancient kabbalists, when the entire truth can be made simple enough for everyone, we will have arrived at the dawn of our redemption. This is why I am so excited about this book. For the first time in history, the nature of Creation and reality can be expressed in a simple fashion. Unfortunately, most of the time when a simple truth is presented to us, it often goes right over our heads; we are conditioned to overcomplicate our lives, to gravitate toward chaos. We have been taught that if something is complicated and intellectually demanding, it must be true. This mistaken notion stands between us and the glorious destiny that awaits us. Remember: the truth will always be simple.

The Beginning

According to Kabbalah, it all began with an endless infinite force called "the Light." Not sunlight, nor the light from an electric bulb. This particular Light is undetectable to the five senses. It is the highest and purest form of Light there is. It is, in its essence, a brilliant, awesome force of energy. Kabbalah tells us that this energy was present at the very *beginning*—before there was any form of physical matter, even prior to the Big Bang and the appearance of the Universe. The *Zohar*, the most important book of Kabbalah, explains that this Light-Force Energy was infinite, unending, filling every corner of reality. It is known as "the Cause of all Causes." In the beginning there was no space or time. There was only Light.

The Substance of Light

This never-ending expanse of Light Force energy is the origin and source of the happiness and fulfillment humankind has been seeking throughout the ages. In the same way that sunlight includes all the colors of the rainbow, the Light that shone before the physical creation of our Universe contained every form of pleasure and fulfillment desired by man. Bear in mind, all these forms of happiness are not the kinds of pleasures we experience with our five senses. These five senses reflect only a microscopic fraction of that original joy, which lay beyond the reaches of the human mind.

This infinite realm known as the *Tree of Life Reality* included immortality, for death and darkness cannot co-exist with Light. The *Tree of Life Reality* is our own true origin and source. This is why we, as human beings, strive 24 hours a day to acquire happiness and peace of mind. This is why we loathe chaos and despise pain. We are homesick, which drives us to tirelessly pursue happiness, unrelentingly, lifetime after lifetime.

Sir Isaac Newton himself said that when the great philosopher Plato wrote about the World of Ideas, he was borrowing those ideas from the ancient kabbalists and their *Tree of Life Reality*. The Platonic world and the *Tree of Life Reality* are similar: in both cases a hidden reality originates everything we perceive in our physical world and every spiritual connection that brings us happiness. Kabbalah uses the metaphor of Light because just as light contains all the colors of the spectrum, the Light in the *Tree of Life Reality* contains all the joy, knowledge, wisdom, and happiness that fulfill us.

At this juncture, students typically raise the question: Where did the Light come from?

The Origin of the Light

According to both Einstein and the esteemed 16th century Kabbalist Rav Isaac Luria (the Ari), the space-time continuum is an illusion. According to modern-day physics and the ancient kabbalistic text, the *Zohar*, the space-time continuum came into existence at the moment of the Big Bang. Prior to this cosmic event, space and time did not exist. Hence, one cannot ask a question that includes the concepts of *before* or *after* when dealing with issues that *precede* the physical Creation. The space-time continuum is an aspect of our physical reality and, as such, it has no place within the realm known as the Tree of Life. Thus, the kabbalists tell us that there is no such thing as beginning or end within the Infinite Realm of Light. The Light was always there. The Light is above the temporal concepts of space and time. Since this removes the relevancy of *beginning*, *middle*, and *end*, perhaps the better question to ask is this: *What is the Source of the Light?*

According to the kabbalists, the Light radiated from a Divine Source that we call *The Creator*, or *God*. The kabbalists make no attempt to discuss God directly but rather they address the *Energy* that emanates from God. The reason for this is logical and simple: the emanation of Light is said to be infinite. Thus, the Light contains all the joy and the knowledge a human being desires, including immortality and infinite happiness. The human mind with its limited rational consciousness cannot even fully grasp the notion of infinity, let alone address where infinity might come from. Therefore, so long as we sojourn in this physical reality, in our finite corporeal bodies equipped with finite brains and rational minds, we cannot delve into the nature of a God who both transcends and emanates the very phenomenon of infinity.

Sun Tan or Sun Burn

This apparent limitation might be compared to the light of the sun. Sunlight provides us all with life. But we don't connect directly to the actual nuclear furnace that is our sun. Instead, it is the rays that emanate from this solar body that give us the energy to sustain life on this planet. We cannot touch the source of the sunlight for, if we did, we'd clearly burn up; we cannot even approach the sun too closely for fear of being incinerated. The solar furnace is far too powerful. But those rays that emanate from this celestial

flaming ball of fire heal, soothe, nourish, and imbue humankind
with life itself, provided we maintain some degree of distance
from the source.

Appropriately, we have found our starting point. Light. It is Light
that is the source and embodiment of pure fulfillment and existence.

THE NATURE OF THE LIGHT

The Light that emanates from the Creator has one singular characteristic: to share, impart, and bestow Its beneficence. In order
to express this nature, the Light created *the Vessel*, an entity
whose sole essence and fundamental nature was that of receiving. All the souls of what would later become humanity—bound
up as one, like cells in a body—formed this great Vessel whose
sole purpose was to *receive* the infinite enjoyment of the Light
Force.

At this juncture there exist but two forces in Creation; the first is
the outward, flowing positive Force of the Light, which in scientific terms may be designated by the (+) symbol, as in a positive
charge or the force of repulsion. The second force is the Vessel,
the receiving entity, the negative charge designated by the (-)
symbol, the force of attraction.

What is emerging from the *Zohar*'s description of Creation thus
far is the beginning of an atomic model, one that preceded modern-day physics by some twenty centuries. The positive Light
Force (+) relates to the positive electrical charge of a proton,
while the negative force of the Vessel (-) pertains to the negative

electrical charge of an electron. These two elementary forces lie at the heart of the physical cosmos, and the kabbalists concur that both forces permeate the metaphysical cosmos as well. Still to come is that mysterious force and subatomic particle that science, as of yet, still does not really understand. I am, of course, referring to the subatomic particle known as the neutron. Together, the proton, electron, and neutron form the atom, the basic building block of our physical Universe.

CONSCIOUSNESS

In our physical, material existence we tend to view energy as a force, a fuel, and a motivating power. However, the energy Light Force referred to by the *Zohar* is also imbued with intelligence beyond measure. In fact, pure consciousness is the very essence and substance of the energy known as the Light Force. The motivating intelligence of the Light Force is the willful thought to share infinite beneficence and goodness with the Vessel. The motivating intelligence of the Vessel is to receive and thus become the recipient of this Divine bounty. Hence, the absolute First Cause in all of Creation is consciousness, specifically the conscious intent to impart unending fulfillment unconditionally. This led to the creation of a second force, the entity known as the Vessel, whose very essence and fundamental nature is the consciousness of absolute receiving. In turn, this led to a perfect relationship, the original Cause and Effect: the consciousness of unconditional sharing of the Light is the First Cause, and the consciousness of the Vessel—which is to receive and enjoy the Light—is the First Effect.

Here we have an ideal, unified relationship known in Kabbalah as *The Endless World,* or *The Tree of Life Reality.* Kabbalah describes the blissful Endless World as a complete, unified entity. Let us now investigate this oneness by way of a metaphor.

HOW TWO BECOME ONE

Imagine carving a bowl out of a large chunk of ice, and then pouring water into the bowl. The water corresponds to the Light and the consciousness of sharing; the ice bowl corresponds to the Vessel and the consciousness of receiving. When we begin to look at this relationship at the molecular level, we see only H_2O molecules. We're witnessing a single reality, even though there are two states here, two opposite intelligences at work—sharing and receiving. On the molecular level we detect *oneness*, yet on another level of existence, the macro level, two opposing states of consciousness are being manifested.

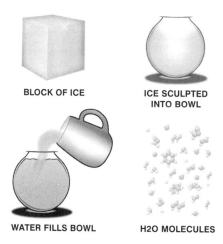

BLOCK OF ICE   ICE SCULPTED INTO BOWL

WATER FILLS BOWL   H2O MOLECULES

On the micro level, the flowing water and the receiving bowl are indistinguishable from one another. The positive (+) intelligence of the water and the negative (-) consciousness of the bowl are impossible to differentiate. This condition provides us with a glimpse into the unity that existed between the Light and the Vessel. It was, for all intents and purposes, impossible to tell them apart. The Consciousness of Sharing and the Consciousness of Receiving were as one.

THE SOUL AS A CELL IN THE COSMIC VESSEL

At this juncture you might be wondering where humanity fits into the cosmic scheme of things. As discussed earlier, the Vessel consists of all the souls of humanity. This includes yours, your neighbors', your in-laws', and all the souls of the world—past, present, and future. All were contained within the one Original Vessel. Once again the concepts and language of science allow us to understand this kabbalistic idea. Science has shown us that a human body is made up of trillions of individual cells. Out of many comes the one. Likewise, the one Vessel was made up of trillions of souls, each soul acting like a single cell in the one Original Vessel, one original soul whose sole purpose was to receive unending fulfillment from the Creator.

**ONE BODY MADE OF
TRILLIONS OF CELLS**

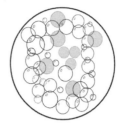

**ONE VESSEL MADE OF
TRILLIONS OF SOULS**

Questions to Be Raised

Why, then, does mankind find itself lost in a disordered world overrun by chaos, an existence riddled with pain and unspeakable suffering? Why are we not all basking in the infinite Light of the Endless World? Why do we find ourselves in a material dimension that knows only decay and death, a reality governed by the law of entropy and the second law of thermodynamics, which states that everything must inevitably deteriorate and corrode over time? What happened to that initial illuminated blissful existence? Where did it go? Where does it hide? Where does it reside now? Where is this luminous realm of perfect order, indescribable happiness, and immortality?

Somewhere along the line there was a disconnection. Humankind lost touch with its true origins. We forgot all about the Light, the Endless World, and the true nature of God. Someone or something erased the deepest memory bank in the human brain, because today these concepts are not as familiar to us as the turmoil on the evening news, the lawlessness in our streets, the conflicts between nations, and the distress that afflicts our ordinary lives.

When one turns to the *Zohar* for answers, the *Zohar*'s response is as shocking as it is profound. Our lapse in memory occurred by design. However, it wasn't designed by the Creator. It was *our own design, our own idea*. The collective souls of humanity requested to have all recollections of the Endless World deleted from our memory. And that, dear reader, is precisely what took place. And as anyone can plainly see, it worked. We haven't the foggiest recollections of life in the Endless World—except, perhaps, for one.

A RECOLLECTION
OF OUR ORIGIN

Why is the pursuit of happiness, serenity, pleasure, and good health an inherent part of our nature? It is because it's a memory. We have tasted it once before. Supposing a tribesman in a remote African village had never tasted a Famous Amos® chocolate chip cookie. Could this tribesman possibly find himself suddenly waking up one morning craving one? Undoubtedly not. We must acquire a taste for something before we can develop a desire for it.

The *Zohar* is clear on this matter: once, we knew what immortality and paradise felt like. This is why the fairy tales we have listened to or told over the centuries conclude with the phrase, "And they lived happily ever after." From the kabbalistic point of view, we do. We will. This is, unquestionably, our ultimate destiny, according to the *Zohar*. And we know this to be true in the very depth of our souls.

Yet for some reason, death, sadness, and extreme doubt about the possibility of a happy ending have come to dominate our human experience. And the memory—*and even the possibility*—of eternal happiness have vanished from our consciousness. This leads us to that all-important question, posed by the kabbalists throughout history: *Why?*

WHY WE FORGOT

Numerous volumes of kabbalistic manuscripts describe the stage-by-stage process that led to the Creation of our world, including the formation of atoms, molecules, and human souls. Kabbalists throughout the ages devoted entire lifetimes to studying these books in order to comprehend the Creation process, much the same way a scientist devotes his or her life to understanding the laws of physics.

The most insightful kabbalistic study is known as the *Ten Luminous Emanations*, which features the gifted and masterly insights of the genius Kabbalists Rav Isaac Luria (the Ari) and Rav Yehuda Ashlag (master of my own teacher, Rav Brandwein). This profound kabbalistic study describes and defines the complete process of Creation. However, here we see one significant difference between Kabbalah and science: Kabbalah's story of Creation can be simplified so that everyone, young and old, can begin to understand *why* he or she is in this world. In answer to the question *Why We Forgot*, the ancient kabbalistic texts offer a simple step-by-step explanation that reveals the following:

- Why the physical world was created.
- Why we are here.
- Why there is darkness and suffering in the world.
- Why we forgot all about the Light in the Endless World.

Though the following will be presented in simple fashion, one should not underestimate the profundity of each concept. When all of this was originally explained by the kabbalists some 2000 years ago, it was called mysticism by the unlearned. Today, we call it science.

INHERITING A GOD GENE

Medical science tells us that genes enable offspring to inherit both physical and personality traits from their parents. Science only penetrated the mysteries of DNA in the 1950s. Obviously, 2000 years ago the concept of genes and DNA would have been unfathomable, but the ancient kabbalists did tell us that when the Vessel was created, it *inherited* a trait from its Creator: the Vessel inherited the potential capacity to share, and a longing to emulate the positive sharing nature of the Light that conceived it.

The Problem of Receiving

Understandably, as long as the Endless World remained unchanged, the Vessel would continue to receive and the Vessel would never gain the opportunity to actualize and express its divine potential. Its innate capacity for sharing would remain dormant, and its longing to emulate the Light would remain unfulfilled. Inasmuch as the Vessel continued to receive from the Light, it could never achieve absolute happiness. This situation also kept the Light from achieving its goal of bestowing unmitigated beneficence upon the Vessel. Clearly something had to change if both Light and Vessel were to achieve perfect happiness for eternity. How could two opposite worlds, two opposing forms of consciousness—sharing and receiving—come together so both could be fully content? How could the Vessel possibly receive and make the Light happy, and in turn, how could the Vessel share to make itself happy? How could these two opposing goals be achieved?

Resolving the Paradox: A Fusion of Opposites

This situation reminds me of what I wrote earlier about my teacher's relationship with both the Labor Union and the Arab peasant.

The secret of my teacher was that he removed all aspects of receiving from his nature. He only concerned himself with giving, no strings attached. He did this with the Labor Union, and he did this with his Arab friend. Rav Brandwein wanted nothing in return for what he gave. My master had no hidden agenda. The *Desire to Receive* was nowhere to be found within his consciousness. In its place was pure unconditional love and friendship. There was no aspect of: *What's in it for me?* As a result, two seemingly opposite entities—moderate and orthodox, Arab and Jew—came together in pure friendship and love.

I didn't realize it at the time, but by giving for giving's sake, unconditionally, Rav Brandwein was emulating the Creator. He had removed all aspects of receiving from his nature. That was the key. By doing so he channeled the Creator directly into the soul of someone who, under normal circumstances, might have been his sworn enemy. If my teacher had even an inkling of self-interest in his heart when he offered the Arab peasant aid and friendship, it would have been a nice, kind gesture. His Arab friend would have been grateful and this nice episode and the warm feelings would have ended right then and there. But that's not what happened. This Arab peasant waited twenty long years to trek all the way to Tel Aviv just to present Rav Brandwein with a heartfelt basket of fruit. The love and joy that this man experienced in sharing this basket with my master was indescribable. The secret was that my teacher removed all aspects of receiving from his nature *first*. That was the prerequisite. Then he offered friendship. Automatically, it was unconditional and pure because all aspects of receiving and self-interest were eradicated. This same consciousness lies at the heart of the solution for the Vessel and, as we'll discover, it is also the key to the practical science of nanotechnology.

My friends, the secret behind the Big Bang Creation of our Universe and the key to immortality is found inside this next bit of kabbalistic wisdom.

The One and Only Right Move

The Vessel had only one choice if it was ever going to experience the joy of giving—to *resist* the Divine Flow of Light, so that it stopped receiving! Once every ounce of *receiving consciousness* is fully restricted and shut down, then the God Gene—the positive *sharing consciousness* inherited by the Vessel—could automatically express itself by blossoming forth. Once again, the student of Kabbalah must ask why.

Essentially, as long as there is even a small trace of receiving consciousness within the Vessel, the Vessel cannot fully evolve to the state of genuinely knowing the sharing consciousness one hundred percent. In its present state, the Vessel is a receiver. The positive sharing trait exists only in potential form. Therefore, the Vessel does not truly understand or grasp the full nature of what sharing consciousness is, despite the Vessel's deep longing to emulate the Creator and share. Wanting to share and knowing how to share are two different things. The only way to master the consciousness of the Creator is to first remove the one stumbling block—the receiving consciousness of the Vessel. With that out of the way, the sharing consciousness of the Creator bursts forth from the God Gene implanted within the Vessel.

Exercising Sharing

The tremendous effort and work required to resist and stop all receiving unleashes the Vessel's divine inheritance. Resistance to receive is the method for activating the unrealized consciousness of sharing. Put another way, if your father is Michael Jordan and you inherit Michael's talent for basketball, you are not going to be shooting three-point baskets the moment you emerge from your mother's womb. We need to exert enormous effort and energy to develop and express whatever innate talent we might possess. Skills, talents, and God-given gifts are always in a state of potential when we are children. We must activate our inner potential through monumental effort, years of training, exercising, and hours of practice. The Vessel's act of resisting this Light—completely—is the workout, the training, and the practice that will allow the Vessel to manifest its God Gene—the sharing consciousness.

The Birth of a New Consciousness

At this point, the Vessel is blessed with a new form of consciousness, the divine consciousness of sharing unconditionally. At this precise juncture something magical happens: opposites fuse and become one.

The kabbalists explained how that magic unfolds. It happens in two steps. First the Vessel must shut down its receiving nature entirely by resisting the Light. When all traces of receiving are eradicated from its nature, the God Gene will automatically spark to life. The consciousness of sharing will awaken fully within the Vessel.

Equipped with its newly birthed consciousness of sharing, the Vessel is now in a position to share unconditionally. It is now identical in nature to the Light. It knows, feels, and tastes the sharing consciousness that now permeates its entire being.

Nevertheless, there is one more hurdle to overcome. The Light Force of God still *wants* the Vessel to *receive* all the goodness that the Light wants to impart. But now there's a remarkable solution to the problem. At this stage, when the Vessel stops resisting the Light and reactivates its receiving nature, this time there is something profoundly different. The Vessel has a new awareness, a new form of sharing consciousness—God consciousness. Now when the Vessel receives, it is actually an act of *sharing*. The act of receiving has been transformed into an active force of sharing.

WHEN RECEIVING BECOMES A FORCE OF SHARING

The *Zohar*'s insight into how receiving is magically transformed into sharing is perhaps the most significant teaching in all of Kabbalah. Equipped with its new consciousness of giving, the Vessel can receive the bounty of the Creator, but this time the Vessel does it for one sole purpose: the Vessel *Receives for the Sake of Sharing* pleasure with the Creator. After all, nothing makes the Creator happier than bestowing pleasure upon the Vessel.

The Master Shares a Tale

My teacher shared a story with me many long years ago that conveyed what is categorically the most crucial principle in all of kabbalistic study. I share with you a variation of the tale below. This simple parable will explain how an act of receiving is magically transformed into a bona fide metaphysical force of sharing. The reader should make every attempt to impress this story deeply into their consciousness for it holds the key to nanotechnology and biological immortality. The story goes something like this:

THE DRIFTER AND THE MISER

Sal Fishman was, without question, the most miserly man in town. He was also very rich, and very arrogant. One evening, as he was leaving his office, he spotted a homeless person camped out on the sidewalk. Normally, Sal was oblivious to such a scene. But on this night Sal Fishman, feeling self-righteous and for his own shameless self-amusement, ungraciously tossed a few coins at the old man as he passed by. But then something happened that Sal never anticipated. The old man handed him back the coins. He politely refused them. "I prefer to earn my own way through life," the old man explained. "But I thank you anyway."

Probably for the first time that he could remember, Sal felt embarrassed, taken aback by the homeless man's obvious dignity. "Look, I'm a wealthy man," Sal responded. "These coins mean a lot more to you than they do to me."

Still, the drifter refused. "Please, don't take it personally," the drifter said. "I appreciate your kindness. But I feel obligated to work my way out of this unfortunate situation on my own. I cannot accept your money."

Goaded now by pangs of humiliation, Sal broke out in a sweat. He was uncomfortable and humiliated in a way he had never experienced before. Sal pulled out a check from his wallet and wrote down a large sum of money and handed it to the ragged old man. He then pleaded with the drifter to accept the charity. Yet the old man remained firm. "I cannot accept it," he declared. "I may not have any money, but I do have my self-respect. Please do not take that away from me. I am sorry but I cannot receive your kind gift. I know you will understand." And that's when Sal became truly mortified, as all his years of self-indulgent shameful behavior flashed before him.

Sal's anguish and pain was not lost on the drifter. Insightful as well as good-hearted, the old man suddenly saw that he had the power to remove the rich man's pain. "Please, sir, I've had a change of heart," the old drifter said. "I will accept your money. And I deeply appreciate your kindness."

To his astonishment, Sal Fishman felt an over-whelming sense of relief, followed by a feeling of deep fulfillment that was indescribable, unlike any-thing he had ever known. And to think he felt this way because a homeless old man had finally agreed to accept a sizable gift of money from him! Sal Fishman shook his head in wonderment at the homeless man on the sidewalk, tipped his hat respectfully, and went on his way.

This story leads us to an important question: Who performed the act of sharing—Sal Fishman or the drifter? By *receiving* the money, the drifter was imparting his own gift to the rich man. In kabbalistic terms, this is called *Receiving for the Sake of Sharing*. When the act of receiving imparts pleasure to the giver, receiving is transformed into sharing. What's remarkable is that, in that moment of sharing, the homeless drifter received what he needed, too. He was able to accept the money without losing his dignity because his act of receiving the money was genuinely an act of sharing. It was unconditional and without a hidden agenda.

Initially, Sal's desire to share was not genuine. Sal did not believe that he, himself, was benefiting by giving the poor man charity. On the contrary, he was feeling self-righteous. His actions were cold, indifferent, smug, and sanctimonious. Sal was *receiving* something by tossing the coins to the drifter. He had an agenda. He was feeding his ego at the expense of the poor drifter. But confronted with the dignified response of the homeless man, Sal underwent his meltdown of shame. Suddenly Sal no longer wanted to feed his ego. He truly wanted to give, unconditionally. And when Sal did so, he received relief from his tormenting pain, followed by the joy of unconditional giving, and new respect for someone he had considered worthless.

Herein lies the ultimate paradox: the moment Sal didn't want to receive something from his action, he was able to receive what he truly needed. Likewise, once the drifter was willing to sacrifice his own sense of dignity for the sake of sharing, he, too, was able to receive both satisfaction at relieving Sal of his pain and a helpful gift of money.

A Constant Circuit of Sharing

What's happening here is a magical expression of Light Force energy. The Light is endless. The Light is Infinite. The Light has continuity, and its sole characteristic is sharing. Both Sal and the drifter emulated the Light by resisting their *Desire to Receive* for their own selfish purposes. Both men shared. And when they did, both men received what they truly needed, as if by magic. Even more paradoxical, the acts of sharing and receiving became identical in nature. That is to say, both were considered the perfect expression of immaculate sharing. The giving action was sharing, and the receiving action was sharing. This became possible once the consciousness of *receiving* had vanished from the scene.

This is a perfect example of circuitry. Two opposites—sharing and receiving—fuse to become one when the *Desire to Receive*—a negative force of attraction—is shut down completely. When both the drifter and the miser completely disregarded their own consciousness of self-interest, their actions were immediately transformed into positive Light Force Energy.

Beneath the Surface

As you can see, it is not the physical action that is important. It is the *consciousness behind* an action that determines everything. We have been conditioned to focus solely on the physical behavior of things, on the surface level as opposed to the underlying consciousness behind a physical property. We will explore this important notion in greater detail a bit further on.

The Goal of the Vessel

Once the Vessel removes all aspects of receiving from its inner being, it ignites a consciousness of sharing. In this new sharing consciousness, the *Desire to Receive for the Sake of Sharing*, the Vessel now realizes that it is sharing with the Creator by receiving the Creator's unending goodness. Also, by exerting a monumental effort to resist and remove all receiving, the Vessel becomes the Cause of its own happiness. How?

The Vessel literally negotiated a deal with the Light saying: *Do not share one ounce of happiness with me until I FIRST resist and stop all receiving.* Under the terms of this deal, the Vessel's happiness becomes solely dependent upon its own effort and work. If the Vessel does not remove its receiving nature, the Vessel will never achieve happiness. Henceforth, the Vessel becomes the sole Cause—and thus the creator—of its own happiness.

Furthermore, when receiving is completely eliminated, and the sharing gene activates, the Vessel can now continue to *Receive for the Sake of Sharing.* Both of the Vessel's inherited desires have now been fulfilled—the Vessel's *Desire to Share* and its *Desire to be the Cause* of its own happiness. Everything hinges on the Vessel's ability to stop receiving for its own sake.

Let us now revisit the Endless World and the most important event that took place in the history of the cosmos—the Vessel's attempt at removing all aspects of receiving from its nature.

THE ACT OF RESISTANCE

The Vessel knew that it now had to stop its *Desire to Receive* completely. This was the first step. And this is the next stage in the process of Creation.

The Vessel literally resisted the inflow of Light. The Vessel said STOP! This act is called RESISTANCE.

VESSEL RECEIVES THE LIGHT

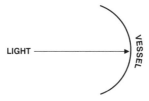

LIGHT ⟶ VESSEL

VESSEL RESISTS THE LIGHT

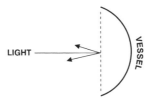

LIGHT ⟶ VESSEL

The Power of Resistance

By resisting the Light, the Vessel is no longer a receiver. It has effectively shut down its *Desire to Receive*. This means the sharing God Gene can now ignite, and the Vessel can reunite with the Light, with both sides happy and fulfilled.

But it's abundantly obvious that we do not live in a world of unending happiness where death no longer exists. On the contrary, we now find ourselves in a world that is the opposite of the reality that we were originally born into. Humankind finds itself neck-deep in a world of darkness where the force of death continues to snuff out our happiness, our joy, the love in our relationships, and, of course, our very lives. Death rules every part of our existence, which prompts the question: *Why?*

The Residue

Imagine pouring milk into a glass. The milk is a metaphor for the Light, and the glass represents the Vessel that receives the Light. If you resist the urge to drink the milk and you suddenly empty out the glass, you will notice something unusual. A small residue of milk remains inside the glass.

This is what took place in the Endless World. When the Vessel performed the act of resistance, it was a courageous, heroic action that blocked out 99 Percent of the Light. But a small residue remained. The only task left for the Vessel was to *resist* the remaining 1 Percent of Light; one more round of resistance was required. However, now that 99 Percent of the Light had vanished, this final round could not take place in the divine illumination of the Endless

World. The withdrawal of the Light left a vacuum, a vacated space, a single circular microscopic point of darkness. The appearance of this microscopic point of darkness marks the appearance of our physical Universe some 15 billion years ago.

THE ORIGIN OF THE BIG BANG

When the Vessel resisted the Divine flow of Energy, the Light withdrew. Consequently, 99 Percent of the Light vanished. What was left behind was empty space, a tiny speck of darkness in a residue of Light. This microscopic speck is our vast Universe. The remaining residue of Light is our sun, stars, galaxies, nebulae, interstellar clouds of dust, hydrogen gas, plasma, and background cosmic radiation that permeates the cosmos. The Vessel's act of resistance and the Light's subsequent withdrawal is the famous Big Bang that astrophysicists tell us marks the birth of the cosmos.

A New World of Chaos

The Vessel now finds itself in an alien Universe. Instead of inhabiting a world of Light, the Vessel resides in a world of darkness. Instead of being in an immortal world, the Vessel dwells side by side with death. Once immersed in a realm of energy, the Vessel now finds itself in a world of dense physicality. After residing in a timeless reality, the Vessel now lives under the influences of the space-time continuum. In this new place, the Vessel would evolve and complete the task of resisting that remaining 1 Percent negative consciousness, and transform.

Finally, in order to accomplish its objective, the one Vessel does something rather spectacular—the Vessel shatters into pieces, producing countless sparks that eventually formed and continue to form the parade of souls that march through time in this terrestrial landscape.

THE SHATTERING
OF THE VESSEL

The event known as the Shattering of the Vessel created the wonderful illusion of *many*. All the scattered pieces of souls could now interact with each other and continue onward with the monumental task of resisting their innate receiving nature while learning how to share. You and I and everyone you know are all individual parts of the broken Vessel, which is our true origin. The work of resisting and eradicating the leftover negative aspect of our nature is a gradual, step-by-step process as we interact with other souls and our environment. It occurs in incremental stages instead of all at once, as did the first act of resistance, for we now find ourselves in a world of time, space, and motion. Every one of the countless sparks of souls in our world is now responsible for contributing its portion of resistance to the overall goal.

How Life Works

Specifically, all these sparks of souls will encounter certain situations and confront other souls who incite selfish reactions. An individual now has two options. He or she can resist this selfish impulse. When we do, that particular amount of resistance is credited to the overall goal of resisting the final 1 Percent. Also, an equal measure of God-like sharing consciousness awakens within that soul. This person now receives a measure of Light Force energy in that one particular area of his or her own life.

In the second option, if the individual does not resist, and instead he or she gratifies the selfish impulse and receives pleasure, life grows a bit darker.

Let's examine this idea more closely, and see how it plays out in the chaotic world that we toil in day in and day out.

PART THREE:

THE STRUCTURE OF EVERYTHING

BIRTH OF THE ATOM

Two atoms accidentally bump into each other.
The first atom says, 'Are you all right?'
The second one says 'I think I lost an electron!'
The first atom says, 'Are you sure?'
The second one replies, 'I'm positive.'

The atom, building block of the cosmos, is a direct byproduct of the shattered Vessel. As discussed in our previous chapter, the Light that emanates from the Creator was always present prior to the Big Bang. The only entity that was ever created ex nihilo was the Vessel. This newly created Vessel had three components. First and foremost, the Vessel embodied the negative-charged receiving consciousness known as *Desire to Receive*. Second, the Vessel inherited the DNA of God, the positive-charged consciousness of sharing. Third, the Vessel had free will, which it exercised when it chose to resist the Light in order to stop all receiving.

It is important to understand this three-fold dynamic well before reading onward. It holds within it the secret for achieving immortality and, as we will discover in later chapters, it lies at the heart of kabbalistic nanotechnology.

The Fall of Atom: Diversity

When the Vessel shattered and fell into the empty vacuum that eventually became our Universe, these three forces of consciousness became denser as they fell from the spiritual reality into a lower state of existence. Positive consciousness became a particle that contained a positive charge. Receiving consciousness became a particle with a negative charge. And the free will of the Vessel thickened into a particle with a neutral force. These three forms of consciousness, in their particle-like existence became the basic building blocks of our Universe—the proton, electron, and neutron—which, in turn, make up an atom.

The electron is the pure material form of the receiving consciousness of the Vessel, which is why an electron has a negative (-) charge. The proton, on the other hand, is the expression of the DNA of the Light, the God Gene, the potential consciousness of sharing that was inherited by the Vessel; this is the underlying reason that a proton possesses a positive (+) charge. The mysterious particle known as the neutron is the embodiment of a neutral consciousness that can willfully choose to resist the Light in order to stop receiving, or choose to continue receiving.

The trillions of atoms teeming in every cubic inch of our reality are the individual pieces of the shattered Vessel. These three types of consciousness found in the Vessel are the fundamental forces at work in the cosmos; from the kabbalistic viewpoint, nothing exists in our physical reality except for these three forces of consciousness. This explains why the entire Universe—in all of its magnificent diversity—is made up of atoms.

These three forms of consciousness, which constitute the complete Vessel, shattered and then filled the vacated space after the Light Force of the Creator withdrew. This is why every speck of matter—from distant stars to microscopic human cells—is composed of atoms and their three components—the proton, electron, and neutron. Atoms rearrange themselves in countless different ways to produce the near-endless diversity and variety of matter, organic and inorganic, that makes up the world that we perceive with our five senses.

Both the scientific community and the ancient kabbalists concur with this view. Science merely employs a different vocabulary to describe these fundamental forces, thereby fostering the illusion that the *Desire to Receive* and the *electron* are two distinct ideas, when, in fact, they are one and the same force.

The Babylon Syndrome

The difficulty in reconciling science and Kabbalah lies in a particular event known as the *Tower of Babel* that took place many centuries ago. The Bible tells us that approximately 4000 years ago the entire world spoke a single language—Hebrew. This shared language provided everyone everywhere with the ability to communicate with one another and thus perceive and grasp the true reality on every level of existence, including the subatomic realm and the metaphysical plane.

From Kabbalah's viewpoint, this means that the scientific-minded, the spiritual-minded, and the philosophical-minded spoke the "same language," and thus each understood—with profound clarity—the truths that each of their respective disciplines possessed. They harmonized their wisdom, which is how they were able to control all levels of the natural and metaphysical worlds.

We're then informed by Scripture that the people of Earth rebelled against the Creator. They set out to build a city (Babylon) and a tower that could reach up to Heaven, thereby giving them the ability to control both the spiritual domain and the material world. The one great strength of these people was their absolute unity, which was so strong that God was unable to prevent them from constructing a tower that could reach Heaven. God's only recourse was to break the unity, which He did by scrambling the language of the people, creating seventy more languages. This event gave birth to all the various tongues spoken in our day and age.

Root of the Science-Spirituality Conflict

According to the kabbalistic perspective on the Tower of Babel story, the Bible is not referring to a physical tower. The tower was a metaphor for a metaphysical technology—including Hebrew letters and kabbalistic methods—that would provide the people with the ability to control both the physical and spiritual dimensions of reality. However, by confusing their language, God saw to it that the people could no longer understand one another or communicate effectively, and this confusion brought a sudden halt to human progress and technology.

The Tower of Babel has repercussions that are felt to this very day. Science speaks one language. Kabbalah employs another. The Koran, the New Testament, and the Torah each have their own particular sacred vocabulary. All these teachings, including the disciplines of science and the doctrines of spirituality, contain truth, but the different languages and terminologies of each discipline foster confusion, conflict, and disagreement. If everyone spoke the same language, they would discover the profound truth underlying all of the world's spiritual and scientific teachings. Unfortunately, this confusion persists.

Physics Discovers the Vessel

For example, in the field of science, physicists have found the point where the negative receiving consciousness of the Vessel materializes in our physical reality. But instead of naming it *Desire to Receive*, or receiving consciousness, they call it an electron, and thus we have confusion. It appears as though we're talking about two distinct entities rather than two different words to describe one force. The result is a false separation between Kabbalah and science.

From the kabbalistic perspective the electron itself is, in fact, a myth. It's just a term invoked in 1894 by G. Johnstone Stoney, who first posited its existence. According to Kabbalah, what science is detecting is, in fact, the consciousness known as *Desire to Receive*. This negative-charged, receiving consciousness is what is real. The electron described by science does not include any aspect of intelligence or consciousness; therefore, science is providing us with an incomplete picture of the subatomic realm.

Kabbalah Discovers the Electron

The *Zohar*, in volume 7, section 83, further develops the idea of the electron or receiving consciousness by telling us that this force initially begins as a wave in the ethereal, microcosmic, metaphysical, or subatomic realm.

> "The World to Come, BINAH, which is called "waves," since everything is found in it in heaps, *LIKE THE WAVES IN THE OCEAN* is from whence they come forth unto all *FACES AND WORLDS*. All the waves and springs come out from the World to

Come, BINAH, to the World of Malkhut, which is called the "daughter of the waves."

As the wave approaches the scale of physical reality, the macrocosm, it begins to assume a more material nature, possessing a negative or receiving charge, giving rise to physicality. (How this wave-particle transformation takes place and the role of human consciousness in this process is beyond the scope of this book.) The *Zohar* goes on to describe this negative receiving force of consciousness as *the daughter of the waves*.

Daughter refers to female, indicating the receptive, negative charge of an electron. In addition, *daughter* represents the birth of physicality, as when a mother gives birth to a daughter. Thus, the term *daughter of the waves* refers to the moment when a wave turns into a negatively charged particle. Physicists provide us with the very same model of the electron, known as the *wave-particle duality*. This refers to the discovery that an electron behaves as both a wave and a particle, mirroring the *Zohar*'s description of the *receiving aspect* of the Vessel that makes up part of our Universe.

Once again, we have two descriptions of a single phenomenon, thereby creating separation between science and Kabbalah.

HUMAN NATURE

The model of the Vessel/atom is also the model of a human being on a spiritual and behavioral level. A human being is composed of three elements, or three aspects of consciousness:

1. the ego/physical body, whose selfish nature is to receive—the dominant aspect of our consciousness;
2. the soul/spiritual essence, whose nature is to share—the hidden, unexpressed, potentially divine aspect of our nature; and
3. the free will to choose resistance, and choose sharing versus receiving.

Some of us are familiar with the idea that there is a Second Voice that attacks our rational mind, influencing this third component—free will. This Voice sometimes appears to have complete control over our thoughts and impulses, thereby making it difficult, if not impossible, for us to choose resistance. Many mistake this Second Voice as their own; never even knowing that this Second Voice even exists, so they allow the Second Voice to undermine their lives.

Unfortunately, we all experience this in our day-to-day lives. Time and again we know that a certain activity or behavior is detrimental to our well being, yet the Second Voice compels us to pursue this negativity anyway—often against our very own wishes. Or we may make a vow to pursue an activity that will undoubtedly have a positive, beneficial effect on our lives; this commitment is genuine, yet the Second Voice raises its ugly head, assumes control over our rational mind, and talks us out of it. The kabbalists, acutely aware of this unique feature of human consciousness, wrote about it at great length.

THE SECOND VOICE DISORDER

The Second Voice is not part of our original consciousness, even though we mistakenly believe that it is. In truth, it's an illusion. It's not you, but a mind trick and a deft deception. The moment you buy into the illusion, it *becomes* you. And then you wind up sabotaging all the effort you've put into a better, more fulfilling life for yourself and your loved ones. You break promises to yourself. You shoot yourself in the foot. You put your foot in your mouth. You step on other people as you climb the ladder of success. You eat things you know you shouldn't eat and do things you know you shouldn't do. Yet, for some reason, you cannot help yourself. The compulsion is overwhelming.

When you finally become fed up, you manage to muster up enough willpower to conquer the Second Voice. Unfortunately, this only lasts a few days, or a few months at best. Then you revert back to your previous habits. Old behavior returns as the Second Voice gets back in command. It stirs up jealousy when your friends, acquaintances, and enemies succeed. The Second Voice blocks out everyone else's opinion but your own. Why does the Second Voice exist, who created it, and what is its ultimate purpose? Perhaps more importantly, why do we not realize that this Second Voice doesn't even belong to us?

THE MASQUERADE COSTUME

When the Vessel shattered into pieces, the shattering created other entities or sparks with which the Vessel could interact. However, the Vessel was not ignorant. Obviously it would know that it was interacting with itself. In order *not* to recognize the other pieces as part of itself, each spark of the shattered Vessel was given a disguise to wear, a costume to create the illusion of *separate and distinct individuals*. This costume is called the ego.

It is the consciousness of the ego that makes us feel that you and I are separate and distinct from the next person. It is a mask designed to prevent us from recognizing ourselves in everyone we meet. If we did, it would be easy to resist the final 1 Percent of receiving and share. But that would pose a tremendous problem for the following reasons.

DEVELOPING THE GOD-GIVEN TALENT

Suppose two people share the same dream of becoming a world-class soccer star. Both individuals possess the necessary raw talent to achieve their objective. One practices shooting goals at an empty net for six months while the other practices by shooting at a net that's defended by a skilled goalkeeper. Which one is more likely to become the more successful player? The answer is obvious. Only when you have an opponent do your talents and skill evolve to their full potential. Lacking an opponent, one can never truly develop their talent to its full promise.

For this reason, the Light created another force of consciousness—referred to as the ego. It attempts to dominate our true self. This allows us to strive against its gravitational pull, and in so doing become the Cause of the joy and happiness that await us at the end of this game. The ego has a singular nature, an unrelenting, ruthless *Desire to Receive for the Self Alone!* The metaphysical DNA of the ego is selfish, unmitigated receiving.

THE ADVERSARY

Knowing and experiencing what it means to share like the Creator has to be earned. And to earn it one must play against a worthy Adversary. The resisting and sharing game cannot be fixed. The risk of losing, season after season, lifetime after lifetime, has to be real—even if it includes death itself! Hence, the Light made the ego—a totally selfish, conniving, self-centered and powerful entity—so that it could offer us a formidable challenge in this game called life.

Kabbalah refers to this egocentric force as the *Adversary*, a term that made its first appearance within the pages of the Bible, specifically the Old Testament and Torah. The word Adversary is translated as Satan in the original Hebrew. From the kabbalistic viewpoint, Satan is not the demonic creature portrayed in religious myth and folklore. He is what his name implies—an Adversary, designed to challenge humankind on the level of human consciousness. The Adversary is a conscious, intelligent force that manifests specifically as the human ego. And it was brought into being for the singular purpose of testing, challenging, and deceiving us so that resisting its influence would be a difficult, near-impossible task. Every thought, every human emotion, every feeling that consumes us throughout our day is caused by the overriding consciousness of the Adversary.

The Selfish Gene

As an aside, the birth of the Adversary within the consciousness of the Vessel is the root Cause behind the celebrated yet contentious scientific concept known as the Selfish Gene, postulated in the 1970s by Richard Dawkins in his bestselling book of the same title. He takes the position that genes are inherently selfish, serving their own interests, and that the human body is merely a gene's way of ensuring its own survival. Kabbalah has no argument with this view. Kabbalah merely takes the idea to the next level, viewing the gene as an Effect and not as the ultimate

Cause; Kabbalah does so by addressing the realm of consciousness.

So, from one perspective, a gene is merely the Adversary's way to ensure its continued existence and to propagate more selfishness in the world in direct accordance with its role of challenging the consciousness of the human soul. Likewise, the human body is merely a vehicle for the consciousness of the Vessel to accomplish its goal of overcoming selfishness. According to the *Zohar*, the existence of the body allows the altruistic aspects of our consciousness to battle the selfish consciousness of the Adversary in one compact playing field—the human body.

The Absent-Minded Soul

It is the Adversary who has caused us to forget our origins, and it is the power of the Adversary to override our consciousness that prevents us from even detecting the Adversary's existence. Compounding this situation are the very doubts and cynicism that we feel regarding the possible existence of the Adversary. Ironically, that, too, is a direct result of his enormous influence over our lives and the entire physical reality. The Adversary blocks out the Light and the truth of his existence the same way a curtain blocks out sunlight from a room.

All of these deceptive shenanigans are part of the free will game, which of course means we also possess the free will to reject all of the above ideas. The ultimate truth about the Adversary is only found in our innermost being. As you read these words, the logic of Kabbalah is filtered through the ego, the first line of defense. This usually launches a barrage of doubt and uncertainty that serves to prevent you from detecting the truth, which remains concealed behind ego-consciousness. This is why many of us conduct an internal debate each time we are introduced to a new kabbalistic principle. Part of us recognizes the power and wisdom of each idea; another part expresses doubt and skepticism.

DEFINING THE HUMAN EGO

Unfortunately, the concept of ego is completely misunderstood by most people. Most of us believe ego refers to that part of our psyche that leads us to behave in ways that are pompous, conceited, self-centered, overly confident, arrogant, and boastful. Indeed, it does. But ego also manifests as low self-esteem. Ego can make you feel worthless, depressed, insecure, timid, fearful, and insignificant. There is one underlying theme in all of the above feelings: thinking only about yourself and your own needs. That is how one truly defines ego. It is about *Receiving for the Self Alone*. In other words, ego means it's all about *me*, regardless of whether the news is good *or* bad.

The Reactive Consciousness

Another way to define ego is *Reactive Consciousness*, the source of reactive behavior. Reactive behavior can come in response to positive or negative things that have taken place in your life. Perhaps you reacted to an insult by losing your temper. Or you may have reacted to a compliment by suddenly feeling pretty good about yourself. In *both* circumstances your feelings were not generated from within your own consciousness; your true soul consciousness was overridden by your ego consciousness, which compelled you to react to an external force—whether it was another person or a set of circumstances. In plain language, when you act on behalf of ego, you are the always the Effect; you are not the Cause.

Reactive Behavior and the Meaning of Life

Reacting to anything is equivalent to receiving. This must be understood before you attempt to read further. Reacting may be defined as negative receiving consciousness. We've learned that we came into this physical reality to resist and stop ALL receiving. If reacting and receiving are the same, we may now rephrase our purpose in life to state that we came here to stop all of our *reactions*. From the kabbalistic viewpoint, this is the meaning of existence. Philosophers have devoted their entire lives over the course of some 20 centuries to a search for that elusive meaning. Incredibly, the student of Kabbalah is able to discover the sole purpose of life after reading just a few chapters of a book. Make no mistake: the meaning of human existence is simple. However, as we know, there is a big difference between simple and easy. As it turns out, the ultimate objective of stopping our egocentric reactions is extremely difficult to attain.

Imagine a day when a few dozen people might pay you some nice compliments. As a result, you begin to feel good about yourself. But then, near the end of the day, one person, who happens to be in a not-so-positive mood, makes a nasty remark about you.

Once again you react, but this time you're upset. It no longer matters how many people had good things to say about you. You are now reacting to the one person who said something offensive. When you react to external events, you relinquish control of your life. All reactions are triggered by your ego consciousness overriding your soul consciousness.

The Purpose of Life

My earlier statement that the souls of humankind came to this physical reality to resist the remaining 1 Percent of desire means, on a more practical level, that we came to resist the reactive impulses of our ego. Each of us who journeys through this physical world has a specific mission; each of us has egocentric reactions that must be resisted and controlled. All the events in our lives—good or bad—are merely triggers to provoke the ego, to elicit a reaction from us. If we react, we miss an incredible and valuable opportunity to resist. If we react, the metaphysical influences of the Adversary and the manipulative powers of the ego become stronger. As a result, the work we came here to do becomes that much more difficult to accomplish. Our life grows a bit darker as the forces of chaos grow stronger. And the endgame, which is the removal of all chaos from this world, is delayed further.

If, however, we learn to resist the ego, allowing it to die just a little bit from the pain we feel by not reacting, we have become proactive. By doing so we have moved closer to the goal of eliminating the remaining 1 Percent of reactive consciousness from our nature, which means we have moved ourselves and the entire world closer to the Light, closer to those elusive goals of nan-otechnology and immortality.

Everything in our lives, all the people (family, friends, enemies included), all the missed opportunities, all the windfalls, they're all an intricate part of a grand obstacle course designed specifically to incite the ego and goad us to react. Everything serves that one overarching purpose. The task at hand for the Adversary, our reactive egocentric consciousness, is to keep us from recogniz-ing the truth—to keep us in the dark about the meaning of exis-tence so that our blood will continue to be shed, and our tears will continue to flow.

Too Simple to Be True?

In the kabbalistic Universe, the goal is to overcome as much self-ishness as possible and to strive to become more sharing, posi-tive people who embrace the idea of giving to others uncondition-ally. For most people, this seems just too simple to be the solu-tion to the problems that afflict this world; it must be too good to be true. Nevertheless, when all is said and done, this is what it all boils down to: selfishness and reactive behavior is the single source of the chaotic, negative forces that devastate the planet and our personal lives.

Relativity

Kabbalah is not, in any way, claiming that each of us must be transformed into a Gandhi, a Mother Teresa, a Moses, or any other sainted soul who dedicates their life to the benefit of others. Such unrealistic expectations are not in keeping with Kabbalah.

Rather, each of us comes into this world with a specific task, a certain amount of resistance (based on our personal situation and previous karmic debts) that can be applied against our selfish impulses. This is known in the language of Kabbalah as *Tikkun*, which means to repair the effects and the seed of prior egocentric behavior. Each of us must achieve a certain measure of change of character. We each have a precise amount of ego consciousness—a particular quantity of selfishness that must be addressed and eradicated.

End Game

The goal of the ego, on the other hand, is to expand our selfishness and increase its influence in our lives. Thus, life serves one great purpose: to oppose the ego and remove as much selfishness and self-interest as possible during the course of our day-to-day existence. When a critical mass of change is achieved, we will have accomplished our goal in life, at which point our personal existence becomes one of unending contentment. Furthermore, the *Zohar* tells us that when a certain threshold is achieved on a global scale, the ultimate task of wiping out the remaining 1 Percent of receiving consciousness (selfishness) will finally be realized. Immortality and eternal happiness will become the new reality in this physical dimension.

THE POWER OF RESISTANCE

The *Zohar* offers the practitioner of Kabbalah a powerful technique for shutting down reactivity. It is called *resistance*. The Vessel originally applied this technique when it resisted the Light in the Endless World, thereby accomplishing 99 Percent of its objective. We are here to complete the balance of the work, which, on a practical level, means *resisting* our selfish desires and impulsive reactions. The ego is not who we really are. It is an illusion perpetuated by the Adversary in order to conceal his presence in our life. It is an illusion so powerful that it motivates us to cheat, rob, backstab, argue, hurt, fight, and kill our own neighbors who, in reality, represent other parts of our soul, for we all descend from the one Vessel.

The Sharing Mechanism

There is one particularly powerful way to carry out resistance throughout the course of one's life, and that is to perform genuine, uncomfortable acts of sharing. Why is a sharing action considered an act of resistance? Receiving is our natural state, and the natural state of the Vessel. However, this innate receiving consciousness has been amplified by the existence of the Adversary—the selfish gene. When we force the body to shift into sharing mode, we are resisting every urge, every reactive desire, and every impulsive longing that typically governs the body.

This is one of the reasons why Kabbalah advocates sharing actions. It has nothing to do with morality, or ethics, or any other noble ideal. Genuine sharing requires an act of resistance, and each act of resistance takes us another step closer to completing the task of attaining 100 percent resistance. Sharing is merely a tool, a means to an end. By sharing with others, we are moving closer to achieving our own eternal happiness. Once again we are confronted with the ultimate paradox: the more we concern ourselves with the welfare of others, the more quickly we will receive the answers to our own prayers, and the fulfillment that will bring us everlasting happiness.

The Art of Sharing

The consciousness known as ego is constantly focused inward, thinking only about *what's in it for me?* Consequently, sharing with another person becomes a nearly impossible challenge. As we've just discussed, confronting this challenge is how we evolve the *sharing gene* that we inherited from the Creator. Sharing is therefore difficult and extremely uncomfortable, which serves the valuable purpose of ensuring that the positive act is derived from an authentic act of resistance.

According to Kabbalah, if you should happen to find sharing an easy task, in all likelihood it is your ego that is motivating the positive behavior—not your soul. Here's a clue: if your deeds of sharing bring you praise, a better reputation, an honorary dinner, a plaque, or your name on the wing of a hospital, this is not true sharing.

A true act of sharing *only* takes place when we override selfishness and greed, when the giver experiences discomfort, and when no other party, including friends and colleagues, knows you performed a positive deed. Extreme self-centeredness and self-interest must *first* be awakened in order for you to reject it and then choose sharing, regardless of what your ego is telling you. This is the root reasoning behind the age-old phrase "Give 'til it hurts." Giving until it hurts is not a moral code. On the contrary, it's a cutting-edge technology, as we'll soon see.

THE TECHNOLOGY OF LIGHT

Light is defined as all the happiness we seek in our lives. The Light is everywhere, infusing every inch of our cosmos, from the outermost regions of deep space to the innermost depths of our souls. Each time you savor a gourmet meal, sip a warm cup of tea, listen to your favorite music, play with your children, become involved in a loving relationship, enjoy a wonderful movie, successfully conclude an important business deal, receive a promotion, snack on Belgian chocolate, soak up the tropical sun, walk in the park, smell a flower, plunge into cool waters on a balmy day, enjoy good times with dear friends, catch a nap on a hammock, invent something useful, compose a lovely song, paint an image, advance knowledge, enjoy an opera, dance, drink, or just take pleasure in any of the simple things of life, you have found the Light. All these good feelings are expressions of the Light Force of God.

What you may find surprising is that you can *also* find the Light each time you scream at your child, cheat on your business partner, take revenge on an enemy, gossip about friends, react with anger, cheat on your spouse, or short-change a customer. If someone robs a bank and he or she derives pleasure from that robbery, that pleasure is also defined as the Light, as controversial as all of this might sound. This is the departure point, the specific place where Kabbalah differs from all other spiritual teachings.

A World without Morals

There are no morals or codes of ethics in the Endless World, or within the teachings of kabbalistic wisdom. The concept of right or wrong is nowhere to be found neither in the Endless World nor within the pages of the *Zohar*. There is only Light in the Endless World, no rules, rituals, or dogma. Kabbalah represents the technology for causing the Light to ignite in our lives.

Before you become confused or angry over this idea of a Universe without morals, consider electricity. We use electricity to power up hospitals, houses, streets, and cities in order to bring comfort and care to people. We can also place our finger in a light socket and electrocute ourselves. In either instance, the nature of the electricity *is the same*. The situation is similar with the awesome Light Force of the Creator. Each of us who travels through this material dimension has the free will to choose *how* we are going to connect to this supreme Force. We can safely plug into the *Tree of Life Reality*, or we can electrocute ourselves. There is no moral dilemma. If you use the wrong technology to connect to this awesome Force, the energy of Light is dangerous. If you utilize the proper technology, the Light enriches your life beyond measure.

Not only do ethics and morals play no part in any of this, there is one human trait that is critical to our technology. It's called greed. Surprisingly, the good old human trait of utter greed can provide a powerful way to draw the beneficence of the Creator into our life. In fact, according the wisdom of the kabbalists, greed should be the *only* motivation behind our behavior. Let's explore this radical notion further.

The Kabbalist Who Loves to Steal

Make no mistake; no one is greedier than I am. No one would rather rob and steal more than yours truly. Rest assured that I am not being satirical or self-deprecating. On the contrary, I am absolutely serious. If I could get away with it, don't think for a moment that I wouldn't love to walk into a bank undetected, and walk out with $10 million in cash. I have been called many things in my life by other rabbis and critics, including charlatan and snake oil salesman. Ironically, they got it wrong. What I am peddling is not snake oil. It's the authentic sacred wisdom of Kabbalah as taught to me by my master and teacher. However, if they had accused me of being a man who often dreamed of robbing Fort Knox, I could not have taken issue with that allegation.

You can be sure that if stealing paid off, if it delivered the goods, if it produced eternal fulfillment, kabbalists throughout the ages would have been robbing banks, hijacking Brinks trucks, and fencing stolen goods twenty-four hours a day. After all, the basic premise of Kabbalah is that we were all created to receive the eternal fulfillment and joy that is the Light Force of God. God shares endless fulfillment. That is the be-all and end-all. God's desire to share this fulfillment with humanity is the quintessential element of true reality. But the fact of the matter is, theft and dishonesty do *not* deliver the goods. Not because of morality, but because of technology. According to the technology of Kabbalah, or the Universal Laws of the natural world, thievery just doesn't work.

PART FOUR:

GREED AND THE LAW OF ATTRACTION

THE LAW OF ATTRACTION

The kabbalistic concept known as *The Law of Attraction* was first discussed in kabbalistic texts some 4000 years ago. It has been described often since then, from the 17th century works of Sir Isaac Newton to the latest book bestseller lists, but there are many misconceptions concerning the dynamics of this Universal Law. Rav Yehuda Ashlag, the teacher of my master, wrote at great length about the Law of Attraction and the dangers associated with not truly understanding it. In fact, this great kabbalist said that until we understand the implications of the Law of Attraction, we will never master the wisdom of Kabbalah. The Law of Attraction is the key to unlocking Kabbalah's secrets, and the code to comprehending its teachings.

Rav Ashlag explains the Law of Attraction as follows: When two things are similar, they are considered to be close. The more similar they are, the closer they will be. When they are identical in form, the result is complete oneness between the two. By the same token, the more dissimilar two entities are, the greater the distance there is between them.

The Light and the Vessel (God and mankind) are separated from one another as a direct consequence of their diametrically opposed natures. The Light shares while the Vessel receives; God imparts blessings while the souls of humankind seek to receive blessings; the Light Force is a positive-charged form of sharing consciousness while the Vessel is a negative-charged receiving form of consciousness.

It immediately becomes clear that the only way to remove the space between mankind and the Light Force of the Creator is to remove the single trait that brings about this condition of separation in the first place. That single trait is *receiving*. We now have discovered a deeper, more comprehensive reason as to why the Vessel needed this physical world to remove the remaining 1 Percent receiving aspect from its consciousness. Once this 1 Percent is removed, the Vessel will automatically establish affinity, connection, and oneness with the Light Force of the Creator by virtue of the Law of Attraction.

WHEN GREED IS GOOD

Kabbalists are a greedy bunch. They make executives on Wall Street look like boy scouts by comparison. But there is one immensely profound difference in their type of greed: kabbalists are greedy for the everlasting Light Force of the Creator, the essence of unending fulfillment. I call this *Enlightened Greed*.

Traditionally, kabbalists have always been shrewd investors in the Game of Life. They are not in any way moral and ethical players in a world overwhelmed with strife. The kabbalist never settles for less; the kabbalist wants it all. He does not want to compromise and settle for a few good years of fulfillment, followed by many years of chaos. The kabbalist wants a continuous upward climb on the ladder of happiness; not a roller coaster ride consisting of pain and pleasure, stress and serenity. Learning how to receive an endless flow of fulfillment is what the Game of Life is all about. This is the thought behind Creation. And we find this truth concealed within the very word that describes these universal teachings: Kabbalah means "to receive."

The mere fact that the word Kabbalah means *to receive* is paradoxical in light of the methodology that Kabbalah champions to help us receive infinite fulfillment in our life: according to Kabbalah, one receives by *not receiving*; we receive by doing the opposite—by sharing.

Enlightened Greed versus Senseless Greed

There are two ways to receive fulfillment from life, and both ways are founded upon greed. Firstly, there is what I characterize as *senseless greed*. This form of greed is motivated exclusively by the metaphysical entity known as the Adversary, or as Ego or receiving consciousness. This form of greed serves to gratify the ego at the expense of the soul. It is a senseless form of greed, for it inevitably cuts you off from the Light Force, the *Tree of Life Reality*, by buying you off with short-term gratification. Why? When you receive you are acting in opposition to the Light. Thus, according to the Law of Attraction, you are creating a greater distance between you and the Light.

To prevent you from detecting the vast distance your behavior has put between you and the Light Force, the Adversary bestows upon you a temporary reward such as ego gratification. However, once that wears off, you inevitably realize that you have wound up falling under negative influences by virtue of your separation from the Light. It will become apparent that this distance creates a space in which chaos raises its ugly head.

The greed that we've called *Enlightened Greed* serves one purpose alone, which is to fulfill the soul with a constant flow of fulfillment at the expense of the ego. Unlike senseless greed, *Enlightened Greed* delivers temporary pain to one's ego but immediately afterwards provides connection to the *Tree of Life Reality*. The infusion of energy that accompanies such a connection serves to diminish the chaos and negativity in one's life. The results are lasting, thus it is a far more shrewd and profitable life choice.

Enlightened Greed means we share, we resist selfishness, and we resist receiving; instead, we emulate the Light of the Creator so that by virtue of the Law of Attraction, our souls achieve closeness and connection with the Divine Energy that fills the *Tree of Life Reality*. For the student of Kabbalah it all boils down to senseless greed versus *Enlightened Greed*, or receiving versus sharing.

Finding Our Free Will

Contrary to centuries of philosophical speculation and debate, mankind's free will lies exclusively at the intersection of these two options. Both the chaos that we experience and the blessings that are bestowed upon us derive solely from our ability to choose which form of greed to serve. What needs to become ingrained into our consciousness—precisely what the overriding ego consciousness seeks to prevent from happening—is that any form of greed motivated by ego will assuredly deliver two results. Initially, you receive pleasure and immediate gratification that is admittedly intoxicating, but temporary; subsequently, a long-lasting negative repercussion will strike when and where you least expect it because of the distance you have put between yourself and the Light.

If this truth were present in our minds each moment of the day, we'd make wiser, more profitable choices in life. This is only achievable if, instead of allowing our ego consciousness to override our soul, we override the impulse of the ego to receive selfishly—that is, if we choose sharing as the more sensible option. Greed for the soul is the willful choice to embrace temporary pain and trauma upon one's ego, not for moral reasons, but because it provides fulfillment that never leaves us.

Unfortunately, I know far too many people who have failed to understand the implications of each of the above principles, even after decades of kabbalistic study. Imagine, if it is difficult for a student of Kabbalah to embrace and live by these truths, how much more difficult it is for the billions of people who have never been made privy to these invaluable teachings. This is the reason the world has been engulfed by conflict, war, bloodshed, and pain for some twenty centuries.

Greed is Not a Problem

For those of us who remain uncomfortable with having the word *greed* used in the same context as spirituality—or Kabbalah in particular—the *Zohar* reminds us that the Creator *thought* the Vessel into existence for one simple purpose—to share infinite fulfillment with the Vessel. Thus, the essential nature of the Vessel is *desire*. This infinite desire is directed toward the infinite fulfillment and happiness that the Light naturally emanates. Kabbalah calls this fundamental nature of the Vessel the *Desire to Receive* or, in contemporary parlance, *greed*.

By *desiring* everything, we are fulfilling God's will, which is to share everything. When we stop desiring the Light, we prevent God's Light from entering into our lives, for the Creator will not coerce us into receiving or being happy. Coercion and spirituality are mutually exclusive. If you force someone to be happy, how can that be defined as true happiness? If you force something upon someone, how can that be considered authentic sharing? God will not impart His beneficence to us unless we first desire it. Desire must be ignited, otherwise the Vessel remains empty. When we do not desire the Light of the Creator with all our hearts, it pains the Creator more than it pains us, because there is nothing that the Creator can do to alleviate our pain and darkness until such time as we awaken a desire for help.

The Real Problem is a Lack of Greed

We roam through this terrestrial plane in darkness for one single reason: a lack of greed. When we desire and crave, we receive a particular form of happiness that fulfills that particular desire. God's Light is now being shared. There is a moment of perfection in the Universe. The Light is sharing and the Vessel is receiving.

However, we have learned that the only way to continually receive the happiness that is embodied in the Light is to first stop receiving and, instead, start sharing. This action provides us with a durable connection to the Light because then our nature (sharing) and the Creator's nature (sharing) become identical in form.

Greed based solely on the *Desire to Receive for the Self Alone* is, in point of fact, the most limited form of greed, for it eventually cuts you off from the Source of all Sources. You receive a small, one-time payment in lieu of unending dividends. If we were greedier people, we'd shut down our receiving consciousness and share unconditionally despite the pain, the doubt, and the skepticism that our Adversary implants within us. This would ensure our constant connection to the Light because now we are emulating the Creator.

This seems so simple that it's almost inconceivable that mankind continues to be governed by senseless greed and ego con- sciousness after so many centuries of bloodshed and suffering. But in all fairness, the world has not been aware of the existence of the Adversary or the teachings of Kabbalah, thanks in no small part to the Adversary himself. It is my whole-hearted desire that this book will resolve that problem once and for all.

The simplicity of the Law of Attraction and of *Enlightened Greed* reminds me of a thought a student once shared with me. The key to putting sharing first is to strive to make it unconditional. In other words, the more you share expecting nothing in return, the more you assume a form similar to the Light of the Creator. When you do so, you draw closer to the Light, allowing happiness and blessings to flow into your life.

Only small-time greed prevents us from going all out.

SETTLING FOR LESS

The difference between a person worth $200 and one worth $20,000 is simply the degree of greed, the levels of their *Desire to Receive* wealth. The individual with the greater desire naturally works harder and longer in order to satiate his or her desire. This individual will not stop until achieving his or her goal, until such time as their desire is quenched.

What emerges from the *Zohar*'s teachings is that every time we settle for the pleasure associated with ego, we are, in fact, settling for less. We think we're being smart, but in truth we're being awfully foolish. We are purchasing swampland in the Florida Everglades instead of investing in valuable waterfront property in South Beach. Why? Because the Adversary launches a full-scale attack upon our consciousness, causing us to believe that we are brilliant players in the Game of Life. Ego consciousness completely blinds us to the exorbitant costs associated with feeding and nurturing our selfish impulses.

As a result of the ego's negative influence, and its deception of our rational consciousness, we believe that the end of death and complete control over the physical, material world is unattainable. We've been led to believe that eternal happiness and paradise on Earth is the stuff of fairy tales and religion. But that's not really what we believe in our heart of hearts. Deep inside we know we are just settling for less as a result of our lack of greed, our lack of desire. Cynicism and fairy tales justify our small thinking and limited consciousness.

The crux of the matter is that we just don't think big enough. We do not set high enough goals. We need to be honest about our situation and recognize this is the underlying problem facing mankind if we ever hope to turn things around. History is full of proof of our limited thinking. If you told people 1000 years ago that we could build a machine to fly hundreds of people around the world, they would view this in much the same way we now view the possibility of immortality and the existence of a *Tree of Life Reality*. At that point in history we did not yet have the capacity or capability to think that big, to dream, envision, and believe that flying machines were within the realm of possibility. Today we are not greedy enough when it comes to such ideas as the end of death and mind over matter. Our small thinking is a direct result of the Adversary's efforts.

The Winds of Change

Today's nanotechnologists are defying this trend, defying conventional thinking by envisioning a reality where nanotechnology can unleash the forces of immortality and physical transformation. The winds of change appear to be sweeping across the planet as new ideas and lofty goals begin to make their appearance in the fields of medicine, biotechnology, nanotechnology, and other sciences. As we'll discover in the chapters ahead, Kabbalah provides us with the missing ingredients, the missing pieces of the puzzle that will make nanotechnology a safe, practical tool and a bona fide reality in our times.

But, in order to achieve this, we must confront our age-old nemesis, for he will not give up without a fight. Shrewdly, the Adversary will provide us with just enough ego gratification to buy us off, to prevent us from desiring something far better than what department stores, Wall Street, car dealerships, or real estate agents can offer us. This ancient opponent tickles our ego so that we feel smart and successful each time we wind up settling for less. Meanwhile, the fires keep burning in the world. We settle for *greed for the ego* and snatch what we can, accepting a short life span filled with chaos instead of choosing *greed for the soul* and aiming for unending joy, happiness, and immortality.

The Small-Thinking Billionaire

A businessperson worth $75 billion is, in fact, a small thinker in relation to the kabbalists of history. Believe it or not, it is relatively easy for the billionaire to have total certainty in his ability to accumulate such wealth. But does our billionaire have the courage and vision to dream about immortality, to set the bar higher and make the ultimate goal, endless happiness, available to all people, without him ever having to worry about what the next guy owns because this next guy's possessions will never diminish what the billionaire now has in his life? It's a tall order, and a complete paradigm shift in human consciousness. One has to be exceedingly greedy in order to think that big, and to make that kind of drastic adjustment in one's thinking.

IT'S NOT ABOUT
GIVING IT ALL UP

Most spiritual doctrines preach self-denial. They teach abstinence. They tell us to give up the material world and our earthly desires in exchange for spiritual treasures. We are encouraged to eliminate our earthly desires. Nothing could be farther from the truth, according to Kabbalah. We kabbalists do not nullify our desire. We do not divorce ourselves from the material world. We do not negate, eradicate, or abdicate our yearnings, for this would stand in direct opposition to the original Thought of Creation, which is to bestow infinite pleasure upon the Vessel. Instead of eradicating our desires, we convert them. We transform them in order to receive what we truly need to make us happy.

Desire to Receive, or greed, must be converted from feeding our ego to feeding the needs of others, which, paradoxically, winds up feeding our own soul and benefiting the entire world as well. In other words, the more we share, the more we receive. Remember the story of Sal Fishman and the old drifter? When our consciousness is tuned into this dynamic, all of our needs will be taken care of by the Universe, as demonstrated by the following analogy.

The Darkened Auditorium

Imagine you're in an auditorium where the lights are turned off, and there are obstacles strewn all over.

There are tall objects to bump into, smaller objects to trip over, and sharp objects that could cut and scrape you.

Imagine that hundreds of other people are locked inside this auditorium with you. Everyone in the room holds one unlit candle. Of course, an unlit candle is of no use, so as they try to make their way through the darkness, they stumble, fall, and continually hurt themselves as they collide with all the obstacles.

All except you. Your candle happens to be lit. It may not throw a lot of light, but it does help you avoid most of those nasty sharp obstacles as you navigate your way around. Once in a while you stumble, but you are far better off than everyone else.

Naturally, you don't want to give away your candle. But, having just finished reading a book on Kabbalah, you realize you must resist your selfishness. So you light another person's candle with your own. And then you realize something rather amazing. You still have your original candlelight. Sharing your flame did not diminish it. This realization motivates you to share a few more times. And then you realize something even more astounding. The light of the other candles is actually helping you to see better, as more and more candlelight illuminates the auditorium.

Soon the people you shared your flame with recognize the benefit of sharing their candlelight. Suddenly, people with lit candles are walking around lighting all the other unlit candles. As more sharing takes place, more light appears in the auditorium. Other people's acts of sharing are generating more light for you. Before you know it, there is so much light in the auditorium, all those nasty objects suddenly become fully visible. At that moment, everyone stops tripping, falling, and hurting themselves. The chaos of the room has been transformed into order through countless acts of sharing.

The more you share, the more Light there is for you and everyone else. Life's obstacles now become visible.

This is life! The lesson is self-evident. And don't be fooled by the simplicity of the example.

The more we share, the more *WE* benefit. We don't have to be motivated by morals, a code of ethics, or a religious authority, for that matter. We can be motivated by *Enlightened Greed*. We can be inspired by our own genuine desire for the Light Force of the Creator. Resisting selfishness creates Light, for it allows us to share. Sharing creates Light—for others and for oneself. It is technology, plain and simple, and it is not in any way based on the idea of noble behavior (which is all too easy for the Adversary to subvert). On the contrary, resisting and sharing is shrewd behavior. When we genuinely realize this, we will have found the secret to a world of never-ending peace.

So why do we tend to ignore all the opportunities to perform resistance and random acts of sharing, if this is our true purpose in life? If sharing and resistance represent the fast track to endless happiness, why do we find it so difficult to remember this truth? Why do we need a book on Kabbalah and nanotechnology to remind us of the meaning of life?

I asked this very same question of my master some forty years ago. The master answered it by way of a story.

The Candle Maker

Long ago, in a tiny village, there lived a fellow by the name of Dusty Rhodes. Dusty could not make a decent living for his family. His wife Sarah and his seven children barely had enough clothes and food. Life was a constant struggle. Dusty's trade was candle-making. He made his meager living walking the streets of his village peddling his candles. The problem was, the village was already crowded with candle-makers, so candles were a dime a dozen. Every day, Dusty would walk miles from dawn till dusk scraping together a few coins. Each night he came home and his wife nagged him about the lousy living that he made, demanding that he find another trade. But candle-making was all Dusty knew.

One day, while Dusty was peddling his wares, the fanciest horse and carriage he had ever seen pulled up alongside him. A prosperous-looking gentleman opened the carriage door and asked to buy a few candles. Dusty could not help but marvel at the plush carriage. The inside was upholstered in the finest velvet. Jeweled pillows adorned the interior cabin. The gentleman could see that Dusty was impressed. He also could see that Dusty didn't recognize him.

"Dusty, it's me, Moe! Remember, I was the water carrier in this village for many years."

Dusty was flabbergasted. "Moe!" he cried out. "What happened to you? Did a rich relative remember you in their will?"

"God forbid," said Moe, "I made my fortune in diamonds and you can do the same!" And that's when Moe told his old friend Dusty all about the mysterious "Land of Diamonds," a tiny island located on the other side of the world. This island, according to Moe, was overflowing with diamonds. Diamonds there were as common as the dirt in Dusty's village.

"Moe, please, I beg you," cried Dusty. "Tell me where it is! I've struggled my whole life trying to eke out a living. How do I get to this island?" Well, that was the difficult part. As Moe explained, there was only one boat that traveled there and the journey took one year each way. That would mean Dusty would be away from his family for four years. As it happened, Dusty's wife had no problem with that.

Many long years of struggling financially had taken their toll on her. A life of wealth was well worth a few years of loneliness. So she told her husband to jump on that boat and bring back the riches.

Dusty did as he was told. He boarded the boat, spent twelve months on the high seas, and finally arrived at the Land of Diamonds. Nothing had prepared him for what he saw. There were diamonds everywhere. All shapes. All sizes. Dusty thought he was dreaming. The streets were literally paved with diamonds. The sparkle of gems dazzled his eyes wherever he went. When he finally composed himself, Dusty started filling up his pockets, then bags, and then suitcases with sparkling diamonds. He then went to a store to buy more suitcases to fill up with diamonds. And that is when he received an unexpected surprise.

When he went to pay for the new suitcases with one of his diamonds, the shopkeeper just laughed. "Diamonds are worthless here, my friend." Dusty immediately understood, and he too laughed. "Of course, diamonds are a dime a dozen here." But then Dusty began to worry. He quickly realized he had no money to pay for the suitcase. He had no money to even buy food, which he would need for the two years before the boat returned. He had spent all his money on the roundtrip fare to the Land of the Diamonds.

Dusty began to panic. When evening arrived, he still didn't know what to do. He was getting hungry and he had no money. And that's when he noticed something very unusual about the Land of Diamonds. Once the sun had set, the place was completely dark. There were no street lanterns. There was not a single candle burning on the island. No one knew anything about candle-making. Could this be true? What an opportunity!

Dusty immediately began manufacturing candles. The good people of the Land of Diamonds looked at a candle the same way Dusty looked at a diamond. They bought them up like crazy. Pretty soon, Dusty couldn't keep up with the demand. So he opened a small factory, hired some people, and trained them in the art of candle-making. Over the next two years Dusty's business grew into a vast empire. He became the wealthiest and most honored man on the island. Everyone loved him. All the citizens respected him. He even began exporting candles to nearby islands, which also had no light.

Dusty took the money that he made from his candle manufacturing and parlayed it into a shipping business so that he could also profit from shipping the candles to other islands. He invested his candle and shipping money into lumber so that he could profit from all the trees being used to build the ships that carried the candles to other islands. His candle empire and its subsidiary businesses kept on expanding.

Finally, after twenty-four months had passed, the boat from Dusty's village on the other side of the world returned. So Dusty gathered up all his riches. He was given a farewell party fit for a king. He then boarded the boat to return to his loved ones and sailed the high seas for another twelve months.

When Dusty finally arrived at his village port, he was filled with excitement. His wife and children ran to greet him. But when they saw Dusty and the boat filled with his riches they nearly fainted. Why? Dusty had returned with a boatload of candles! Candles were everywhere: in his pocket, in his hundreds of suitcases, in giant containers loaded on the boat. He must have brought home a million candles. Of course, these candles were worth billions on the other side of the world. But here, back at home, they were worthless.

Dusty Rhodes had gotten so caught up in the temporary world he was in that he had completely forgotten the reason why he journeyed there. He had forgotten what was truly valuable to himself and to his family. And if you think Dusty's wife nagged him before this incident, you can imagine how she berated him for the rest of his poverty-stricken life!

Our world is the Land of Diamonds. And just like Dusty, we have forgotten why we came here, which is to resist our selfish desire, to identify and uproot *all* of our negative reactive traits, to starve the ego, and to share. Each time we receive for its own sake, we wind up with a worthless candle. Each time we share, we gain a diamond.

You may be surprised to hear that every negative trait that we possess is a valuable diamond! And each positive trait is a worthless candle. Why? Negative traits provide us with the opportunity to resist, and thus finish the job we came to this world to achieve. But we've forgotten why we are here. Consequently, what do we do all of our lives? We look for praise and honor for our positive traits. We seek attention for all of our fine attributes and show them off to everyone. We ignore and deny all of our egocentric negative traits, not realizing that they are curtains that hide the true wealth that can fulfill us beyond our wildest dreams. We extol our own virtues to everyone we meet. "Look at all the good I've done." "I am such a good person." "I am too nice to people." "Look how smart I am."

We are not very good business people in this Game of Life. Instead of snatching priceless diamonds and filling our pockets with them, we grab for worthless wax. Perhaps we can finally wise up and realize that it's time we all started getting greedier. Shutting down our ego and resisting all our reactions is the greatest form of greed there is.

PART FIVE:

CONSCIOUS-NESS AND THE CAUSE OF DEATH

DEFINING SHARING

As we discussed in an earlier chapter, true sharing means we are selfish *first*. It means that initially we despise the thought of giving to another person. Then, in the moment that we resist that overriding selfish consciousness and we give anyway, we accomplish a true act of sharing and, in turn, remove a portion of the 1 Percent remaining reactive consciousness from our nature. The *Zohar* tells us in no uncertain terms that sharing is a difficult task. For it to be real sharing it must be uncomfortable, and it must include a genuine change of nature.

A Second and More Significant Way to Share

Each time you identify and admit to having one of your selfish traits, this is also considered a profound act of sharing. Again, this is difficult. But when we admit our jealousy, envy, insecurity, and selfishness, we automatically put ourselves in a sharing state of consciousness. We are in a proactive state of being. This effort is considered to be a major contribution towards the overall goal of completing the final act of resistance.

Hence, when Kabbalah says we must learn how to share, it does not only refer to giving money, time, and effort to a worthy cause, or to a friend in need. It concerns something far more difficult. It means we admit to our best friend and our enemies that we are green with envy over their good fortune. When we do that, we remove a part of our ego. We eliminate a portion of the leftover 1 Percent receiving consciousness from our essence and take one step closer to the promise of immortality.

THE CAUSE OF DEATH

According to the *Zohar*, death is the culmination of a lifetime of reacting, and of service of the ego. However, with ample evidence pointing to cancer, heart disease, stroke, car accidents, and murder as the culprits, how can we accept such a seemingly simplistic kabbalistic explanation? Furthermore, *how* does the ego become the perpetrator of death? This is such a radical notion, such a major transformation of consciousness, that it will initially be difficult for the rational mind to fathom, thanks in no small part to our Adversary. So let's take a closer look at the dynamics of death.

The Law of Attraction and the Angel of Death

One way to understand why death occurs is through the Law of Attraction. Our entire world, from the smallest subatomic particles born in the world's most powerful atom-smashing particle accelerators to the people who populate our planet, is sustained by the Light Force—the unseen energy that emanates from the Creator. Each time we react, each time we receive for its own sake, we are acting in opposition to the Source of all life. In so doing, we disconnect and distance ourselves from the Source of existence. Eventually that distance becomes too great, and we reach the moment when our disconnection from the Source is complete.

This is death. Thus the Angel of Death might appropriately be renamed the Angel of Disconnection, for this is the underlying cause of death. Disease, heart attacks, car accidents are merely the physical manifestations, the external expressions of our disconnection from the Source of all Life. Our spiritual disconnection is the *Cause*; physical death by whatever circumstance is only the *Effect*.

Now let us begin by exposing an illusion concerning what happens to the Light when we die.

The Energy Remains

Although disconnection from the Light results in death, the Light of the Creator, the source of our life force, constantly shines. Think of electricity, which is constantly present in your home even though the light of a lamp is extinguished when you pull out the power cord. Furthermore, the Light Force never changes, even as our lives seem to be steadily consumed by an ever-increasing amount of darkness and chaos.

This is precisely what humankind has failed to comprehend over the centuries. People lament, cry, and wonder aloud: *Where is God?* The truth of the matter is, God never left. The Light never changed. It continues to shine from the perspective of the *Tree of Life Reality*. It is only in our world, as a result of the distance we have created between ourselves and the Source of Light, that we fall victim to the illusion of change.

This distance—which is caused by our continual behavior in opposition to the Light—might be likened to a series of curtains. If one places a curtain in front of a light source, the room grows darker. Additional curtains make it darker still. Eventually, adding more curtains will darken the room completely. This is death. But the light source remains constant. Only from our perspective does the room appear black.

RECONNECTING TO THE ENERGY SOURCE

The obvious way to increase the quantity of light in our darkened room is to do away with the curtains. Therein lies the crux of our problem. Our natural tendency is to chase after the Light, to chase after fulfillment, happiness, and even life itself when we are stricken with a fatal illness. But we are, in effect, chasing after the wrong things. Light, happiness, healing, and the life force are always present. It is the curtains we've erected that block out these intangible qualities from our lives. Rather than chasing after the Light, we must find and identify all the curtains that conceal the Light that is always there. We must transform the traits that are responsible for creating that distance. Those traits are found within the reactive ego consciousness of humankind. These negative traits are the curtains that bring about aging, sickness, disease, and ultimately death. The reason we have failed to find lasting happiness and immortality is we've been going in the wrong direction, taking the wrong route.

Enlightened Greed as a Tool for Transformation

As I mentioned earlier, a kabbalist refuses to react, refuses to be selfish out of greed. The kabbalist knows that a measure of death energy—a curtain—will block out the Light of the Creator, creating further distance between God and ourselves. Every unkind deed and reaction increases that separation. A kabbalist, however, wants it all, and knows that only the Light can offer it all. Therefore, a kabbalist devotes his entire life to drawing closer to the Light by imitating the Light throughout the course of his or her life.

This becomes the kabbalist's sole motivation for kind, proactive behavior, for admitting all of his faults and negative qualities, no matter how shameful or painful they are to acknowledge. For each identification and admission of an egocentric quirk brings us closer to the Light.

The Way of the Kabbalist

Over the centuries, kabbalists and their cadre of students would spend hours each day pointing out each other's faults. Each student committed himself to accepting—unconditionally—the criticisms, barbs, insults, and critiques of their colleagues, friends, and most especially their rivals. Whether or not the criticism was warranted made no difference. It was about weakening and diminishing the ego, the primary stumbling block to a life free of chaos and death.

A true kabbalistic master knows which buttons to push to ignite the ego of his student. A loving and learned friend knows precisely what will trigger reactive behavior in his dear companion. It was a precise art, because if you trigger too strong a reaction, if you hurt one's ego beyond a certain point, the student will call it a day and walk away from the path. Touching the raw ego is a far more painful experience than a dentist drilling on a raw infected nerve.

Students of Kabbalah would devote their entire day to serving their teacher, serving one another, and performing extraordinary acts of sharing. They subjected themselves to a routine of constant uncomfortable giving, out of pure *Enlightened Greed*. They sought the greatest treasure of all—immortality. They understood that everything in this Universe depended on their behavior toward one another. They knew that the Angel of Death—which we will expose shortly—could not touch them unless they allowed him into their lives.

Students of Kabbalah did not need a code of ethics to motivate them to *Love Thy Neighbor*. They had a firm grasp of the nature of reality. They understood nanotechnology. They saw how life and death worked, and they saw what no one else could see— the hand of the Adversary behind the actions of humankind.

These practitioners of Kabbalah knew the sole purpose of the Adversary was to convince us that the teachings of Kabbalah were untrue. After all, it's so much easier to cut out a tumor than it is to cut out a nasty character trait. With this in mind, let us now reveal exactly what the great masters and students of Kabbalah understood about life, death, immortality, and nanotechnology. Thanks to the latest developments in science we now have a language and the means by which to explicate the methodology for attaining immortality via kabbalistic nanotechnology.

PART SIX:

THE HEART AND SCIENCE OF NANO-TECHNOLOGY

A CONCISE RECAP OF KABBALISTIC COSMOLOGY

We've spent a great deal of time understanding the creation of the world and the meaning of life, as stated by the master kabbalists of the past. The purpose behind this was to lay a foundation of understanding so that we may begin to grasp the dynamics of nanotechnology through the eyes of the kabbalists, and thus discover a technology for bringing about the end of death. Toward that end, allow me to recapitulate what we've learned in the preceding chapters, for without a firm and clear understanding of these ideas, it will be difficult to comprehend the profound connection between Kabbalah and nanotechnology.

Once Upon a Time

In the beginning there was Light. Not physical light but a positive-charged Force of Energy, Divine Consciousness, filled with infinite happiness and an incalculable sum of knowledge, emanating from a hidden, unknowable source known as God. The *Zohar* explains that the Light's sole essence was *unconditional sharing,* so the Light created a second form of consciousness, a perfect receiver, to be the Vessel that desires and delights in the infinite happiness. Therefore Creation—prior to the Big Bang—consisted of two exclusive intelligent forces: a positive energy force (God's Light) and a negative energy force (the Vessel's *Desire to Receive* the Light).

We discovered that this Vessel—though a pure conscious force of receiving—inherited the DNA of its Creator, the God Gene. Accordingly, the Vessel was unhappy. The Vessel wanted to share like the Creator, instead of just receiving; the Vessel wanted to give instead of take. It sought to transform its God-given receiving consciousness into an opposite state—a positive instead of a negative, a sharing consciousness instead of a receiving consciousness. This presented what seemed to be an insurmountable problem, because the Light wanted the Vessel to receive but the Vessel only wanted to share.

Fortunately, the Vessel discovered a way out of its dilemma.

Birth of a Cosmos

The first step toward a solution involved a powerful act of resistance on the part of the Vessel in order to stop receiving the Light. After the Vessel rejected the positive-charged rays of Light, the Divine Energy vanished, leaving an empty space, allowing for the Big Bang that gave birth to our Universe. However, there was still a residue of Light remaining within the Vessel, leaving the Vessel to complete the final 1 Percent act of resistance by shutting down every trace of receiving from its consciousness.

The Birthing of Positive Light-Based Consciousness

Once the last 1 Percent of resistance against receiving consciousness is complete, the inherited positive consciousness of the Light (DNA) will automatically materialize within the Vessel. At this stage, the Vessel will be in a position to *reactivate* its receiving consciousness, but this time there will be a profound difference. The Vessel's conscious act of receiving will have been completely transformed into a conscious force of sharing. At first this sounds paradoxical, for how can a consciousness of receiving also be considered a consciousness of sharing? How can a negative charge also be considered a positive charge? How does a minus (-) become a plus (+)?

THE 1 PERCENT SOLUTION

We can understand the solution to this paradox by turning again to the tale of the homeless drifter and the wealthy miser, Sal Fishman. As you will recall, the drifter's act of *receiving* the miser's money was transformed from a receiving action to a sharing action for it imparted relief to Sal, who desperately sought to remove the intense shame he was feeling. Thus, in this particular situation, the action of receiving became a true act of sharing.

The Sharing Process Continues

In turn, by *sharing* with Sal Fishman, the drifter also received the financial assistance that he needed all along. He accomplished this by not focusing on receiving but rather, by *Receiving for the Sake of Sharing* with Sal. The drifter's consciousness was directed exclusively by the desire to impart relief to the suffering Sal Fishman, and because of this the drifter was able to share and at the same time receive financial aid with his dignity intact.

And when Sal truly gave from his heart he received comfort, relief, and dignity, because it gave such tremendous delight and enjoyment to the drifter, who wanted to see Sal relieved of his distress. So Sal gave the money to the drifter and received comfort and relief at the same time.

Endless Loop

As we discussed, what we have here is an endless loop of sharing, a continuous circuit of positive energy as the *negative force of receiving* literally disappears due to the overwhelming sharing consciousness and benevolent mindset of both the giver and the receiver. Though there are two parties performing two distinct actions—sharing and receiving—in point of fact there is only *one* action taking place: the act of sharing. This is how two opposites come together to create a unity bond and remove any distance between them.

In the lexicon of Kabbalah this extraordinary phenomenon of endless circuitry translates into the dictum *Love Thy Neighbor as Thyself*. When you love your neighbor in this way, there is no conscious act of receiving or taking; both parties are sharing and thus emulating the perfection of the Light of the Creator. This is how two people bond together, according to the kabbalistic Law of Attraction, which dictates that **like attracts like and opposites repel**. Everyone shares and, as if by magic, everyone receives what they truly need.

A TALE OF ATOMS

My teacher shared the story of the homeless drifter and wealthy miser with me some four decades ago—not to teach me the morality of sharing or the decency of charity—but rather to prepare me for the assignment he bestowed upon me so long ago in Jerusalem. That assignment involved bringing the kabbalistic secrets of immortality to the world.

The story of the relationship between Sal Fishman and the homeless drifter was, in fact, a code, a kabbalistic metaphor for the chemical bonds that exist between all the atoms in our Universe including, most importantly, the atoms that make up the human body. In addition, it held the secret for uniting our physical world with the unseen spiritual dimension known as the *Tree of Life Reality*, the ultimate source of immeasurable happiness and the incalculable sum of all knowledge.

I was astonished by this revelation and started to appreciate the profound, mind-numbing implications of what Kabbalah could offer mankind. However, only with the advent of nanotechnology in the scientific community, did all the pieces of the puzzle fall into place, providing the language and context for sharing the greatest of all kabbalistic teachings.

THE BONDS OF IMMORTALITY

We know that atoms are effectively immortal, based on all scientific research. The atom never undergoes decay; it never ages or decomposes. Incredibly, atoms that were present during the time of the Big Bang—some fifteen billion years ago—are still with us today, as immaculate and flawless as they were the day they were born. The only elements in our Universe that disappear are the molecules.

When two atoms hold hands, they are now a *molecule*. This is like the workings of an alphabet. When letters of an alphabet join together, the letters are now called a *word*. When *words* join together they are now called a *sentence*. However, the moment that *space* is introduced into the system and it separates the basic elements—in this case, the letters—the meaning of the word and sentence disappears. Its meaning and structure have vanished. Nevertheless, the basic components and building blocks of the system—the letters—still exist.

LIFE

When the letters are bonded together they create a word.

L I
E F

When the bonds break and space separates the letters the word no longer exists, but the letters still do.

Likewise, when atoms stop holding hands, the molecule dies, but the atoms continue to live on. When atoms bond together they form molecules, which then bond together to create physical matter. Our hearts, livers, brains, muscles, tissues, and bones are all made up of molecules. When molecules die off, the organs in our body begin to deteriorate and age. But the atoms that created the molecules that made up the organs of our body live on forever.

Hence, according to the kabbalistic point of view, there is no such thing as real death. **Death is an illusion caused by space.**

Space: The Final Frontier

Earlier, we renamed the Angel of Death, calling it the Angel of Disconnection. Permit me to alter and refine this name further in an effort to more accurately express the kabbalistic perspective of death: a more specific term would be *The Angel of Space!* The emptiness that we define as space is ultimately what causes a human being to cease to exist, a topic we will cover further on. From the kabbalistic view, it is the idea of space that ultimately separates atoms from one another, causing the disappearance of the human body.

When the human body undergoes death, all the atoms that originally formed the body are separated by space, however, the atoms themselves are alive and well. They remain immortal after the body decomposes and simply circulate back into the environment.

Hypothetically, if the atoms were reconstituted into their original bonds and patterns, the body would reappear. What kinds of chaotic forces prevent the atoms from assuming their prior connection that formed a perfectly healthy body? What force stops the recycling and reconnecting of atoms that, year after year, continue to form the defined structure that is a human body? What influence keeps the atoms apart over an expanse of time and space, thus creating the illusion that the body no longer exists, when in fact it does, at least in terms of its constituent atoms?

Science tells us that the second law of thermodynamics (which I shall refer to here as the Second Law) plays a key role. In a nutshell, the Second Law describes how energy gradually dissipates, molecules increasingly separate and move apart, and the Universe tends toward apparent disorder. Why does the Second Law exist, according to Kabbalah?

LOSCHMIDT'S PARADOX

History always repeats itself.
—Proverb

On September 5, 1906, the great Austrian physicist Ludwig Bolztmann committed suicide. It happened while he was on summer vacation. Depression had overtaken the renowned physicist, who today is considered a giant of science. Ironically, one of the contributing factors to his depression was the fact that the scientific establishment did not eagerly accept his ideas. Boltzmann's colleagues in physics did not agree with his view that matter was made up of molecules and atoms. Clearly, Boltzmann was a man ahead of his time.

Ludwig Boltzmann was a colleague and close friend of Johann Josef Loschmidt, another notable Austrian scientist. Through their combined work in chemistry and physics, along with contributions of Henri Poincaré, a bewildering paradox emerged that has become known as Loschmidt's paradox.

They found that, in our world of the five senses, the world we touch and observe, the second law of thermodynamics and the arrow of time give us the sense that matter and energy deteriorate over time and that this deterioration always occurs in a forward-moving direction. We perceive this effect every day. Hot coffee becomes cold as the molecules/energy/heat dissipates. Yet, for some reason, the reverse never seems to occur: a cold cup of coffee never heats up on its own. A window shatters, but the reverse never seems to take place, where all the atoms suddenly reconfigure into their original state.

However, Henri Poincaré demonstrated that, given enough time, a molecular system would eventually return to its original state. It might take trillions of years, but it would happen. It is *time* that creates the illusion of irreversibility, and thus the illusion that things tend to move toward entropy, disintegration, and decay.

Today, simple computer models confirm Poincaré's theories. With just a handful of simulated molecules, you don't need a trillion years to witness the return of a molecular structure to its original state. It happens in less than a minute. The question is this: Why does so much time have to pass in our macro-world for this phenomenon to occur, when in the microscopic world, the reversal of entropy can happen so quickly?

The Forest Fire

For instance, in a forest fire, all the atoms and molecules of the trees are dispersed into the air as a result of the heat generated by the fire, as per the Second Law. The forest vanishes accordingly. Following Loschmidt's and Poincaré's line of thinking, one could ask, why can't the atoms and molecules suddenly reverse their motions and come together again, causing a lush green forest to appear? Or, in the middle of a fire, as the atoms of the trees are dispersed and rearranged into smoke and ash, why couldn't they naturally come together again so that smoke and ash produce a forest? After all, both are made up of the same raw atoms. Conceivably, it could happen.

Once again, the traditional view of science, in accordance with the Second Law, was that the flow of atoms and molecules—from tree to smoke, to ash and apparent chaos—could not be reversed and thus tended toward separation and the deterioration of matter/energy. But according to Loschmidt's paradox, the concept of irreversibility (which means molecules *cannot* be reversed) is not consistent with the laws of physics, which state otherwise. On the microscopic level, molecular motion could indeed reverse, thus allowing molecules to return to their original state, allowing our forest to conceivably appear out of nowhere.

The Heart of the Paradox

On the level of the microcosm—the world of atoms and molecules—time does indeed flow both ways. Molecules can reverse. Yet in our world of the five senses, of our everyday experience, this never happens, leading to the paradoxical question: How does a system where time reversal is a constant reality give birth to a system where irreversibility is a statistically improbable occurrence?

In simpler terms, our world is made up of molecules and atoms. If the molecules and atoms that build us can reverse in time, why can't we? Somewhere along the way—from the world of atoms to the world of people—there appears an illusion that time cannot be reversed. No one has been able to bridge (and bond) the two realities.

Part of the Solution

In accordance with kabbalistic practice, I will first give a partial answer as to *why* this illusion is necessary. One simple reason the Universe was created as it is, under the illusion of the existing space-time continuum, is so that, statistically speaking, human beings would not be able to witness forests appearing out of ash and smoke or long-dead relatives materializing out of molecules in the air on a hot summer day. Time and space, as we know it, create the illusion of irreversibility and the near impossibility of witnessing a recurrence of a previous molecular state. This allows us free will as we attempt to complete the task of resisting, of striving against the apparent forces of turmoil in order to learn how to create our own order out of the chaos, thereby expressing the God Gene we inherited from the Creator. Instead of having paradise handed over to humanity carte blanche, the Vessel wanted to become the Cause and creator of its fulfillment.

The one-way flow of time is necessary for free will. I will explain precisely how time and the Second Law account for free will later on. In addition, I will reveal the elegant and staggering solution to the question of why the microcosmic world and our familiar material world exhibit opposite properties concerning the one-way flow of time and the movement toward disorder versus a two-way flow and a state of increasing order.

Let us now return to the idea of *space* as the underlying culprit behind death.

THE CAUSE, NOT THE EFFECT

Though the following kabbalistic perspective may be counter-intuitive, one should know that the space that exists between atoms is not a result of atoms breaking their bonds; it is not a consequence of atoms no longer holding hands. On the contrary, the *space* (which we'll soon define) is the underlying Cause of atoms letting go of one another. Space is the Cause and the broken bond is the Effect, as peculiar as that may seem.

Conventional logic dictates that when two atoms holding hands suddenly let go of each other their bond breaks, and as a result there is a gap, a separation between the two. However, what emerges from the *Zohar* is the precise opposite viewpoint. The *first* appearance is that of the space—the intelligence of separation—and it is *this* intelligence that is the underlying Cause of two atoms letting go of one another. This paradigm shift in logic is critical if one is to grasp and apply nanotechnology.

Space and Separation Originate in Consciousness

The injection of space between two atoms first occurs within the realm of consciousness. It is consciousness that weakens and eventually snaps the bonds between atoms. This is something that we might call *Separation Consciousness*, which is nothing more than receiving, or selfish, consciousness. This is what breaks the rhythm of the cosmic dance and dynamic interplay that naturally exist between all the atoms in our Universe. Before we delve further into this rather exotic kabbalistic notion, we must gain some understanding of the chemical bonds that bind individual atoms.

This book is not intended to be a discourse in science geared toward physicists or scientifically-minded readers. On the contrary, this book is meant for lay readers, for those of us who seek the removal of pain and suffering from the landscape of human civilization. Therefore I will necessarily use broad strokes when explaining the bond between atoms and Kabbalah's views of this phenomenon.

TWO BASIC BONDS

Science tells us that atoms form two different kinds of bonds—one is termed an *ionic bond* and the other is called a *covalent bond*.

Ionic Bonds

Let's first examine the ionic bond. All atoms want to be *happy*. This is the term chosen by scientists, although a kabbalist would say that it is no coincidence that science is using *happy* to describe the inner workings of the atomic and molecular worlds.

Suffice it to say, atoms want to be happy. They want to become stable. How? Atoms have an outer shell provided by electrons as they *orbit* the nucleus of the atom (usually in pairs). Suppose a particular atom requires eight electrons in its outer shell in order to be happy and stable, but it only has six. This atom is not happy, because it lacks two electrons. Suppose a second atom also requires eight electrons in order to be happy, but that atom happens to have ten electrons in its outer shell. We now have one atom that is short a pair of electrons and another atom that has one pair too many.

Sharing and Receiving Electrons

According to science, these two atoms will seek each other out and an exchange will take place. The atom with the two additional electrons will share them with the atom that is short two electrons. After this give and take, both atoms will now possess eight electrons and both will be happy. Now something happens. These atoms bond together to form a molecule, in an exchange called an ionic bond. On the surface, there was an exchange, giving and taking, sharing and receiving, which led to a bond between the atoms, producing a *molecule*.

Opposites Attract or Repel?

These two atoms remain bonded after this exchange because of their respective electrical charges. According to the science that we learned as children, opposites attract. At first glance, this appears to be the case with our two atoms. When our second atom with the additional two electrons shares them with the first atom that was short two electrons, that second atom becomes positively charged. The first atom that receives the two additional electrons now becomes negatively charged. Thus, according to science, opposites are attracting—(-) and (+)—and this is why the two atoms bond.

This conventional scientific interpretation of opposites attracting seems to violate the Kabbalah Law of Attraction, which states that *like attracts like and opposites repel*. If the ancient masters of Kabbalah tell us that *like attracts like*, how would they explain the bond between the two atoms, one positive and the other negative?

THE SOLUTION

In actual fact, Kabbalah concurs with science when it states that we perceive an effect where opposites attract. However, the effect of opposites attracting is just that—an Effect. Science is focusing on the Effect in this physical world rather than the underlying Cause. In our physical world of effects, opposites do attract. But in a higher reality, a more elemental reality than the subatomic world, like attracts like.

The World inside an Atom

Science, accepting the concept of *opposites attracting*, tells us that the electron in one atom is attracted to the proton in a second atom, and this is why the two different atoms bond. Kabbalah takes the position that, although this is the apparent effect on the physical level, it is the opposite effect on the level of consciousness where *like attracts like*. The obvious question to now ask is: Why doesn't the electron in one atom attract the proton within the atom that both are inhabiting?

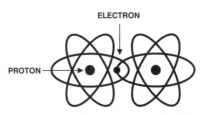

**According to science, two atoms bond because
the electron of an atom is attracted to the proton of another atom.**

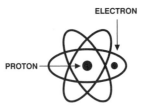

**Why then, isn't the electron of an atom attracted to the proton
of the same atom if opposites attract?**

In other words, if science claims that the law of *opposites attract* operates between two separate atoms, why doesn't this same law operate within a single atom? What keeps the electron separated from the proton in the nucleus?

I believe Kabbalah explains that phenomenon using its insights into the laws that govern true reality: on the deeper level of consciousness the electron is repelled from the proton in the nucleus of the atom that they both inhabit due to their opposite natures. The Law of Attraction is the singular force behind the fact that atoms don't collapse in on themselves.

A Microcosm of Creation

Furthermore, the electron's distance from the proton in a single atom mirrors our distance from the Light of the Endless World. It is a reflection of the relationship between Light and Vessel, which are now separated by virtue of their opposite modes of consciousness—sharing versus receiving. The Vessel shattered into countless particles, falling into the vacuum that is our Universe to interact with other shattered pieces of the Vessel for the sole purpose of nullifying its receiving consciousness, transforming into it into a consciousness of sharing.

Thus, a single atom is a microcosm of this condition. The electron in one atom will not try to consciously bond with the proton in the same atom, nor can it because of its opposite charge. Rather, the single atom only interacts with other atoms—bits of consciousness—learning how to share and receive, with the end goal being to utilize the *receiving force* (an electron) only for the purpose of sharing.

This mirrors the behavior and the objective of the macro-level consciousness—the individual. This is how people bond.

The Consequence of Failure

When an individual is consumed with extreme selfish consciousness and acute negative behavior, the electron's distance from the proton in its own atom will become so great it will break free from the atom. This condition creates what medical science terms a *free radical*, which is responsible for considerable mayhem within the body. But more about free radicals a little later on.

THE SECRET OF NANO

The Art of Atomic Bonding

The *Zohar* says we are here to transform our *Desire to Receive* into the *Desire to Receive for the Sake of Sharing* (where *receiving* becomes a sharing force like the act of the homeless drifter). On an atomic scale, the electron is merely a force of consciousness that Kabbalah designates as the *Desire to Receive*. When an atom shares an electron, the force known as *Desire to Receive* is being used for the purpose of sharing. In the language of science the *electron is being used for the sake of sharing with another atom.*

A Second Option

However, there is another way for atoms to exchange electrons. An atom can dump its electron upon another atom for the purpose of making *itself* happy. This is the opposite of the consciousness of sharing an electron and helping a neighboring atom become happy and stable. There is a profound difference between the two. Consciousness and thought is what makes the difference. Your actions either serve your (*Desire to Receive*) or they serve another (*Desire to Receive for the Sake of Sharing*). In both cases we are dealing with electrons, or the negative charge (-) known as *Desire to Receive*.

BONDS: WEAK OR STRONG

If an atom *shares* an electron for the purpose of fulfilling the need of its neighboring atom, it means a transformation has taken place from the *Desire to Receive* into the *Desire to Receive for the Sake of Sharing*. But if an atom is *unloading* its electron to fulfill its *own* desire, the transformation never happened. This is still *Desire to Receive*.

Receiving Becomes Sharing

This formula also applies to the second atom that receives an electron. There are two ways to receive: one is to *Receive for the Sake of Sharing*—helping the donating atom achieve its own balance (see Fig. 1). Or, the atom that is short an electron decides to *rob* an electron from a neighboring atom (see Fig. 2). It is the same action but from a very different mode of consciousness.

(Fig. 1)
An atom receives the electon
for the sake of sharing with the
donating atom.

(Fig. 2)
An atom robs the electron from
a neighboring atom.

Remarkably, when you peruse science books and websites that describe methods of atomic bonding, some say atoms *lose* electrons, *rob* electrons, or *fight* over electrons. Other books and websites tell us that atoms *share* electrons or *happily receive* electrons. These terms are not coincidental. Atoms are made of consciousness, the same consciousness that coined these descriptions.

There is No Real Atom

Atoms mirror our consciousness because atoms *are* our consciousness. They are not separate. There is only one idea here, one entity being discussed—*consciousness*. Each atom in our body functions in unison with our consciousness and behavior, whether we share for the sake of helping others or resist an act of selfishness (also an act of sharing). The first atom shares its electron to fulfill the need of its neighbor, which is short an electron. And the second atom receives an electron from the first atom to assist it, for the first atom had too many electrons. Both are now expressing the same positive force of sharing, and therefore, through the mechanism know as *like attracts like*, they form a powerful bond. If the consciousness of both atoms is dedicated only to meeting their own requirements, the bond between them is weak and thus more vulnerable to outside influences.

Behavior Controls our Atoms

Behavior is born of consciousness. When we are reactive and selfish in life, our reactive, selfish *macro-force* of consciousness resonates with the countless atoms that make up our body. This consciousness now underlies and influences a great number of chemical bonds throughout our body. As our consciousness changes throughout the day by virtue of our actions, so too does the bond between our atoms. The condition of every chemical bond depends exclusively on our behavior—reactive versus proactive, selfish versus selfless, egocentric versus humble, angry versus calm, victim versus accountable. This is, without question, a revolutionary moment in our understanding of how the human body functions.

The Origins of Disease

Our consciousness, expressed through our behavior and actions, determines the quality and strength of the bonds in every atom in our being. Selfish egocentric consciousness undermines the bonds, disrupts the healthy recycling of atoms in our body, and makes us vulnerable to the environmental influences of illness and aging.

In the simplest of terms, when we're reactive, living a life governed by self-interest, our atoms resonate with this same intelligence. They will tend to want to dump (instead of share) their negative load (electrons) on neighboring atoms to make *themselves* happy and stable. When the negative consciousness of one group of atoms is the opposite of the sharing consciousness of neighboring atoms, their atomic bonds are weak. Their opposing natures repel each other, inevitably leading to separation and *space* between atoms on the physical level.

AS ABOVE, SO BELOW

The most important shift in human awareness and understanding that can take place is for humankind to realize that as space comes between people, space comes between our atoms. How we interact with others reflects how our atoms interact with one another below the surface of our organs, tissues, and cells. Our behavior and the behavior of our atoms are ruled and motivated by a single flow of consciousness.

The Power of *Love Thy Neighbor*

If we were capable of completely and selflessly *loving our neighbors as ourselves* with all our heart and soul, atoms would bond and dance forever, and our bodies would never age or die. Now we begin to realize why the great masters of Kabbalah tell us that *Love Thy Neighbor* is a technology. It is based on the understanding that it is our consciousness that controls the interplay, the interaction, the bonding, and the recycling of atoms that take place in our bodies, which means our consciousness, determines the quality of our health and of our existence.

Covalent Bond

Water's main feature is the fact that its atoms bond through a process called covalent bonding. In this scenario atoms share their electrons with neighboring atoms (see Fig. 3). This is the ultimate expression of *Love Thy Neighbor as Thyself* and helps explain, kabbalistically, water's unusual properties.

(Fig. 3)
COVALENT BOND
Two atoms share their electrons, thereby making both happy and stable

Chances are good that you drank a glass of water today. What you probably did not know is that you swallowed a three-billion-year-old beverage. The water you sipped has been around for billions of years. If you ever accidentally swallowed a large mouthful of milk that had passed its expiration date by just a few days, you will appreciate the profundity of this fact. The water we drink was not processed in a factory and has no expiration date. This multi-billion-year-old liquid never spoils. Water has other properties that make it the most unusual liquid in the Universe and it is these mysterious properties that account for the very existence of life.

The *Zohar* says water is the closest substance on Earth to the Light that radiates from the Creator. In fact, often when the Old Testament and the *Zohar* speak of water, they use the word as a metaphor for the Light Force of the Creator.

From the kabbalistic viewpoint, all of this is due to the consciousness of water, reflected in the covalent bonds between its atoms. Science confirms that covalent bonds are the strongest of bonds.

Divine Reflection

A covalent bond mirrors the ultimate purpose of life, which is to share unconditionally with one another, where the receiving force (electron) of each person (atom) is perpetually utilized for the single purpose of sharing. In other words, in this ideal situation each of us is utilizing our innate drive and ambition for success (this drive being the electron) to fulfill other people's needs; since the rest of the world is focused on fulfilling *our* personal needs, we will no longer have to worry about our own requirements. Sharing becomes the only reality. This is immortality.

When we master the covalent bond, spiritually speaking, death ends; there are no more expiration dates, thanks to the unique power of the covalent bond. Now, from the cosmic perspective, there is perfect affinity between the Light and Vessel. According to *like attracts like*, our world remains bonded and eternally connected to the *Tree of Life Reality*.

Why then doesn't the entire world start sharing at this very moment? Why don't we commit ourselves right now to using all of our talents, gifts, ambition, drive, and desires (all these traits being the electron) for the sake of helping others to become happy? Wouldn't this create a cosmic covalent bond between our physical world and the spiritual world? Would this not bring about immortality?

Simple but Not Easy

The answer is simple: *yes*. However, it is not easily achieved for the following reason: there is a second force of consciousness lurking among us. This is the Adversary, whose intention is to convince us that selfishness pays off, and that he does not exist. Furthermore, he is making it difficult, at this very moment, for us to truly wrap our minds around everything we have just read. Thus, we have to work at defeating him first, and therein lies the greatest challenge to mankind. This is what resistance is all about. This is the reason to resist self-interest, jealousy, and anger, and the reason to embrace caring. This is why the essential teaching underlying the Torah, the New Testament, and the Koran is *Love Thy Neighbor.*

The only enemy that the Torah, the New Testament, and the Koran speak about when they call for the destruction of our foe is the Adversary and the enemy within us—the selfish ego. But the Adversary compelled us to misunderstand these biblical directives, so we have fought external enemies instead. This is why death is still with us, in all of its various manifestations. Space between people, nations, and different faiths creates space between the very atoms that give rise to our existence and support our lives.

HOW PROBLEMS AND CHAOS ARISE

It is incumbent upon the human race, being the biggest piece of the shattered Vessel, to accomplish the final task of resisting the remaining traces of receiving consciousness. According to the *Zohar*, when we refuse to accept this obligation, our consciousness has the ability, due to the size of our internal Vessel, to override the entire Universe, thus affecting the inanimate, vegetable, and animal kingdoms on a subatomic level. Thus, it is our actions that cause deterioration, decay, and death in the rest of the world.

FREE RADICALS AND REACTIVE CONSCIOUSNESS

For quite some time now, free radicals and antioxidants have been popular subjects when it comes to the topic of aging and disease. Kabbalistically, free radicals and antioxidants are simply manifestations of our reactive consciousness (free radical) and sharing consciousness (antioxidant) on the atomic level. Let us find out how this works.

The Free Radical

Science defines a free radical as an atom that loses an electron, leaving the atom with an "unpaired" electron (electrons are most happy and stable when paired in an atom). The atom with the unpaired electron is now very reactive, and the free radical will steal an electron from a neighboring atom. They will fight over it and usually the free radical wins. Now the losing atom is transformed into a free radical, so it then swipes an electron from another neighboring atom. This ignites a chain reaction, creating millions of free radicals, and things begin to spiral out of control.

Free radicals damage everything they touch including tissues, cells, and even DNA, causing faulty translations of genetic material. This damage causes aging, many major diseases including heart disease, certain cancers, and rheumatoid arthritis, and of course, it eventually causes death.

The Antioxidants

Antioxidants are happy, stable atoms and molecules that can stop the dangerous domino effect caused by the voracious free radicals. How? Unlike other atoms, antioxidants do not become reactive when a free radical steals their electrons. The antioxidant remains stable even after losing an electron. Therefore, if our bodies have enough antioxidants to share their electrons with the free radicals, the dangerous chain reaction stops dead in its tracks. Everyone is happy.

The problem arises when our bodies suffer from a significant imbalance—an overabundance of free radicals in relation to antioxidants. Now the free radicals are free to run wild and rob electrons, causing all kinds of damage to the body, with no countering force to stop the chaos. This is why the body ages and falls victim to disease.

It never ceases to amaze me how the *Tower of Babel Effect* continues to cause confusion, forcing us to overlook the profound simplicity of what is really taking place. Instead of using complex words like free radical (which is merely an unstable atom with a voracious appetite for other atoms' electrons) and antioxidant (which is a stable atom who's happy to share its electron), we could articulate the situation as follows:

> *Once upon a time in a splendid neighborhood, a very greedy and reactive atom burglarized one of its neighbors and robbed its electron. The victimized neighbor became reactive, and stole an electron belonging to one of its other neighbors. This third victimized atom also reacted badly to the situation. It swiped an electron from a neighbor who was minding his own business. Pretty soon everyone was reacting in the same manner, stealing from everyone. The whole neighborhood was rapidly deteriorating. Parks and public utility buildings were being destroyed as the greedy atoms turned into hooligans, destroying everything in their path.*

> *Everyone understood that their own behavior was self-destructive, ruining the neighborhood in which they lived, but they couldn't help themselves. They just kept stealing from others. They tried hypnosis,*

self-help books, and a change of diet, but nothing worked. Then one day along came an atom with a different consciousness. Instead of robbing electrons, this atom happily shared its electron with one of the greedy atoms. Suddenly, the greedy atom was happy and the sharing atom was happy.

More and more sharing atoms moved into the neighborhood and started sharing their electrons. Suddenly, the robberies stopped. Just like that. Soon the neighborhood was restored to its previous splendor, as all the other atoms recognized the value of changing their response to the greedy atoms. Instead of reacting, they decided to share their electrons with any atom who wanted one. And so they all lived happily—and non-reactively—ever after.

What emerges from the simple story of the Free Radicals and Antioxidants in the neighborhood is the reason both our societies and our bodies fall apart. Our consciousness and behavior toward others is what kills us. There is no such thing as a free radical. It's only selfish receiving consciousness being manifested at the most elemental level of our body's reality.

This form of negative consciousness, when it manifests in our minds and is expressed through our behavior, destroys our neighborhoods, cities, countries, and world. There are *not* a myriad of causes behind the internal and external problems that plague us on a personal, social, and global scale. There is only one, states Kabbalah. The one cause is consciousness. Consciousness creates free radicals and antioxidants on every level of existence.

This might explain why some studies have suggested that the free radical/antioxidant theory is flawed, while the vast majority of scientific studies confirm it. Let's examine this contradiction, and see if we can resolve it.

It's *Not* the Foods We Eat and It *Is* the Foods We Eat

Almost all scientific studies over the last few decades confirm the dangers of free radicals and the benefits of antioxidants. But a few studies suggest there was little change when antioxidants were increased in a patient's diet. How could people who eat foods high in antioxidants still die of cancer or heart disease? According to Kabbalah, it's because their consciousness did not change. Kabbalists never just eat food. Kabbalists consumes *energy*, or *consciousness*, when they eat, in order to strengthen or alter their own consciousness. Kabbalists use various techniques (such as blessings) to awaken the consciousness and Divine energy that is contained in everything we eat.

For instance, we're told that blueberries are one of the most powerful antioxidants. Kabbalistically, what this means is that blueberries, like everything else in this Universe, are part of the shattered Vessel. As we learned, the Vessel has three forms of consciousness: *Sharing*, *Receiving*, and *Free Will*. The *Zohar* explains that when the Vessel shattered into countless pieces, each of the nearly infinite number of Vessel particles contained its own particular blend of these three levels of consciousness, depending upon where it originated in the Vessel.

Some pieces primarily came from the sharing consciousness aspect of the Vessel. Other pieces derived from the middle part of the Vessel, and thus contained a more balanced measure of sharing and receiving consciousness. And there are pieces that issued predominantly from the negative, receiving side of the Vessel. Irrespective of what part of the Vessel physical matter is derived from, *all* physical matter—from blueberries to zebras—is part of the shattered Vessel.

Thus, if blueberries are powerful antioxidants it means their atoms (which represent their inner consciousness) accrued predominantly from the positive sharing aspect of the Vessel. Hence, a blueberry contains a higher concentration of positive consciousness energy, which translates into higher levels of *antioxidants* or *sharing atoms*, all three being one and the same. Poisonous mushrooms, like any food that is detrimental to our health, are simply pieces of the Vessel that stem from the most concentrated sections of the Vessel's negative receiving consciousness.

Thousands of years ago, the great master kabbalists composed the so-called *blessings* that appear in ancient biblical texts specifically to awaken and activate the conscious energy of the foods we eat in order to release those forces of consciousness within the food and, in turn, within ourselves. Perhaps a better word than blessing—which carries the baggage of religious connotation—is *activator*. In fact, the Adversary shrewdly corrupted this activation methodology and turned the idea of blessings into sacred words of praise and worship for the Creator—as if an omnipotent and beneficent Force needed or desired our praise and worship. Imagine a father putting bread on the table for his beloved wife and children, and then demanding praise and worship from his family before they ate!

You Are What You Eat and Think What You Eat

Nevertheless, if an individual does not know that it is, in fact, consciousness that he or she is ingesting, if one doesn't utter the kabbalistic activator that ignites the consciousness of the blueberry, then the individual is not deriving the spiritual nutrients of the food he or she eats. He or she is capturing 1 Percent of the physical nutrients that are available, gaining physical fuel and nothing more.

Similarly, if you consume exorbitant amounts of antioxidants, but you are not aware of the consciousness behind the food, and you remain reactive and self-centered in your behavior, your antioxidants will have no effect because they do not exist for you. Antioxidants are forces of positive sharing consciousness and if you shut that consciousness down, if you override it in favor of negative consciousness, you have unleashed free radicals. You can eat blueberries and gobble up antioxidants to your heart's content, and they will have no effect. As Karen, my wife, soul mate and teacher always says—*it's not what you put into your mouth that matters but what comes out of your mouth.*

When eating foods like blueberries, if you understand their *consciousness content* and *spiritual nutritional value* your goal should be to eat them in order to strengthen your *ability* to resist selfishness. Food is a gift from the Creator to nourish us physically and, more importantly, spiritually. It is a means of transferring the *consciousness* of the Creator into our being so that we develop the strength to resist reactive behavior and share, emulating the Light Force that radiates from God. The more we emulate the Light, the closer we draw to it. The Law of Attraction!

Cause versus Symptom

If we eat food with the intent of capturing its consciousness and thereby enhancing our own, we are treating the cause of our problems. If we eat foods only to influence the state of our physical bodies, we are only treating the symptom, and there will be no genuine wellness. If a change does occur, it's because the person was somehow motivated to change their behavior at the same time they chose to change their diet, which is often the case when people decide to change their lifestyle.

THE POWER OF WATER

Let us now consider the covalent bond as an example of the importance of consciousness. Kabbalah tells us that, prior to the Flood and the story of Noah, water on Earth had divine properties. Drinking water not only nourished but it also healed, resurrecting ailing or dead tissues and cells simply by imbuing its sharing consciousness into the consciousness of the atoms in the body. This is why the early biblical characters in the Old Testament lived as long as 200-300 years of age, with Methuselah living more than 900 years. The secret of their longevity lay in the power of water.

However, when the Adversary (ego consciousness) assumed control of the people, this affected the consciousness of the water. After the Flood of Noah, the consciousness of the waters was corrupted and remains so to this very day. The covalent bond is still present but the consciousness behind the bond has changed.

The natural, divine state of a covalent bond looks like this (see Fig. 4): on the physical level, the two atoms are bonded together by shared electrons. Both atoms achieve stability and *happiness* exclusively through the conscious act of sharing. Each atom offers its electron to the other, and both wind up with two electrons, making the atoms happy.

(Fig. 4)
COVALENT BOND
Two atoms share their individual electrons with one another thus providing each two electrons.

In water that is corrupted by human consciousness, the covalent bond works as follows: on the physical level, the two atoms are bonded together by sharing their electrons; on a higher level of reality, the consciousness level, the intent of both atoms is to rob an electron from its neighbor (see Fig. 5). Neither side wins the *tug of war* so the two electrons hover between the two atoms; this is the nature of their bond.

(Fig. 5)
**Atoms fight over each other's electrons, reaching a
stale mate, thus producing a negative-based covalent bond.**

Many scientific studies have demonstrated that our conscious thoughts can influence water. When one realizes that over 70 percent of our bodies are made of water, one can begin to understand how consciousness could be the cause of all sickness and disease. Covalent bonds, hydrogen bonds, and water play a critical role in our DNA. If our bonds are weak, an opening is created for the possibility of corruption in our DNA code.

Consciousness determines whether the bonds are strong or weak. Once we recognize that this is the sole determinant of our health and well being, we are on our way to achieving nanotechnology and, in turn, immortality.

PART SEVEN:

THE HEART
OF THE
MATTER

ADDICTED TO MATTER

Science, in its never-ending quest to probe to the fundamental level of reality—from physical matter to molecules, to atoms, to electrons, to quarks and leptons, to photons—has stopped short of the ultimate source. This is not the fault of science as a whole, but rather a direct result of the tireless labors of the Adversary, who ignites fear, anxiety, and hesitation within the scientific community as it approaches the level of reality that leads directly to *consciousness*.

It seems as though Science has always been uncomfortable moving beyond the realm of physical reality, even though its discoveries in the twentieth and twenty-first centuries have moved us further and further from a world consisting of fixed matter, and into a Universe made up of probabilities. It is the Adversary who keeps scientists and lay people addicted to matter.

The Fear of Letting Go

Science and technology have participated in the phenomenon of shrinking physical matter by delivering more and more power through smaller and smaller packages. Today's laptops have far more computing power than massive, room-sized mainframe computers of just a few decades ago. Large networks of telephone cables have been replaced by razor-thin strands of fiber optics. Still science clings to the shrinking units of so-called matter. It keeps reducing physical entities to smaller and smaller constituent parts (from molecules to atoms to protons to quarks, etc.), finding in the process an almost endless array of exotic new subatomic particles. But it is still not ready to cross that proverbial line in the sand and step into the realm of consciousness.

Ironically, the scientific establishment seems "religious" in its reverence for physical laws, despite the counter-intuitive paradoxes emerging from the fields of quantum physics. Just as fear and peer pressure maintain order in the ritualistic, dogmatic world of religion, so too do they keep the scientist devoted to physical laws. But when the truth is ready to be embraced, immortality will be available to each and every one of us. And it could happen in this lifetime.

The Search for Truth

According to Kabbalah, as long as science keeps smashing atoms in the quest to discover the First Cause, the Ultimate Source of existence, it will look forever. The *Zohar* is clear on this: the path from pure consciousness (The Endless World) to the illusion that is physical matter (our material Universe) contains infinite stages. Therefore the only practical way to reach the Ultimate Source is to take a quantum leap and discover what the kabbalists demonstrated over twenty centuries ago: consciousness is the basis of all we perceive and all that is; it is the source and ultimate root of reality.

Consciousness is the Vessel shattered into incalculable numbers of particles that populate the entire subatomic realm. Consciousness is who we are. Could it be a coincidence that the three forces of consciousness that reside inside the Vessel are identical to the three forces that reside inside the atom?

HOW TO FIND THE TRUTH

Consciousness is the basis of all things physical. But you find it *only* when you *make the choice* to find it, only when you choose it. Your own individual consciousness is what needs to be utilized in order to find the consciousness that lies at the root of all existence. What does is it mean to utilize one's consciousness? To answer that question we must ask what consciousness is. This in turn is a question that philosophers and scientists have explored and debated throughout the millennia, and the kabbalists are no exception.

DEFINING CONSCIOUSNESS

In order to find the truth, we need to rise above the influence of the Adversary, who embodies doubt and skepticism. Rising above doubt by recognizing the existence of the Adversary is *part* of consciousness. And behaving in a manner opposed to the influence of the Adversary is a means of achieving a higher state of consciousness. This is the elevated state of unconditional love, of unequivocal sharing, and of absolute caring for another person. It is the highest form of consciousness, for it is identical to the consciousness of the Light, the Source of *all* consciousness.

To *not* recognize the Adversary's existence or his influences is to be controlled by him. This is not conscious behavior; this is reactive robotic behavior. Reactive behavior doesn't preclude intelligence, and intelligence is not consciousness. Intelligence is knowledge. Consciousness is unconditional love.

One can be both intelligent and devoid of love for others.

Unconditional love imitates the consciousness of the Light and thus creates unification. The Light is the source of all consciousness, therefore when our consciousness is like that of the Light we achieve the highest possible level of consciousness, which is infinite in all aspects. It includes infinite fulfillment and the sum of all knowledge.

The Path to Raising One's Consciousness

Consciousness is awareness and self-awareness. Therefore, if you are not aware of the existence of the Light Force of the Creator (the Source of all intelligence and consciousness) and the presence of the Adversary, then you are not aware of your complete self, and you are lacking in consciousness. You might be a genius, intellectually speaking, but you are lacking in consciousness. We can be smart and miserable, and we can be of average intelligence and happy and fulfilled beyond measure. The greater our awareness of the Adversary, and the more we separate our thoughts and actions from his, the higher our consciousness will be.

In summary, the Light is the source of all consciousness. We are merely a Vessel with the ability to receive and contain that consciousness. The objective of the Adversary is to prevent us from drawing the Light (consciousness) into our being by convincing us that he doesn't exist.

What is the nature of the consciousness of the Light? *Sharing. Unconditional giving, and the desire to impart to others.* What is the nature of the Adversary? Self-interest and reactive behavior. The more our behavior emulates the Light, the higher our consciousness will be.

The Adversary, our ego, makes us feel smart, clever, and arrogant, so that he can maintain his iron grip on our lives. He allows us to use intelligence to satiate our desires so that we won't seek out consciousness or detect his existence, which would lead to his demise.

When we wake up and genuinely recognize that consciousness is the root of reality, we will have risen above the Adversary. That is the moment we find the absolute truth.

The Secret to Finding the Truth

Kabbalah reveals that we came into this world to become more pure, more sharing, and more unconditional in our caring for others, not to become smarter or more intellectually astute. True consciousness is unconditional caring and sharing. This is the formula that leads to nanotechnology and immortality.

The Deceit of Doubt

Kabbalists tell us that the Adversary embodies the very DNA of *doubt*, for it is the very nature of doubt to doubt its own existence.

In other words, we are innately disposed to put forth intellectual arguments that discount the truths presented to us—including the fact that we have doubts! We do not realize that doubt underlies every aspect of our argument. The most that we can discover this way is intelligent, lucid, convincing information that relates only to the Effect—never to the underlying Cause.

THE ULTIMATE DOORWAY TO TRUTH

The *Cause of all Causes* and the highest of all truths is only found when we transcend self-interest, overthrow the Adversary, utilize our souls, and allow our care for others to become our sole motivation. Believe it or not, this can be achieved right now with one simple shift in consciousness. If we can just open up and admit for a moment that everything we've done in our lives thus far has been based on self interest, if we just admit the possibility of the Adversary's existence, that one simple difficult step turns out to be a giant, quantum leap forward into the realm of truth. That is when a door opens wide. That is when the fabric of space-time unzips before your very eyes, and you peer into the heart of reality to discover...*consciousness staring back at you!* At that glorious moment, consciousness has found consciousness.

Blessed with this pure consciousness, we reinforce our understanding that total sharing is the path home, the path to the Light, and the route to immortality. We have resisted the Adversary to reach this point and now we choose to share 100 percent (*Love Thy Neighbor as Thyself*), for we know what this will bring us. We now are emulating the consciousness of the Light to perfection. And when we bond completely with the Light, death meets its demise almost gently. Herein lies the ultimate meaning of the phrase *raising your consciousness.*

Prior to this moment in history, the path to truth was supposed to be a gradual process, a step-by-step, ever-increasing awareness that an Adversary indeed exists. We had a choice of choosing pain or choosing enlightenment through spiritual transformation. History has shown us that humankind has continually chosen the path of pain and has refused to learn the necessary lesson. But now we can choose inner transformation simply by altering our consciousness. Here's how: initially, we must find a way to climb out of the abyss of crushing doubt, which is a formidable task. But that's what this book will allow you to do. Once that difficult first step is achieved, you will climb up a ladder of mounting certainty until you reach the level of absolute knowing. It can happen as quickly as you allow it to. Each time we resist skepticism and selfishness, we advance another rung of the ladder toward a higher level of consciousness.

This is why the kabbalist lives a life embodied by resistance. The kabbalist seeks ultimate truth and contact with true reality. Once we attain that elusive 100 Percent awareness of the Adversary, we will resist him 100 Percent. We'll embrace total sharing and grasp the mystery of *Love Thy Neighbor.* At this lofty level of consciousness, physical and spiritual immortality will be realized for all humanity.

Recognition and continued awareness of the Adversary and the Law of Attraction will prove to be the final puzzle pieces in achieving what is unquestionably the Holy Grail of science, the accomplishment of a Grand Unified Theory, otherwise known as the *Theory of Everything*.

THE SEED OF OUR ADDICTION

I, myself, have often wondered what led science, and all mankind, to its addiction to matter. My teacher provided me with an answer four decades ago that shook me to very the foundations of my soul. Today, some forty years later, his response continues to resound deep within me as I pose a question that all readers should now be asking themselves: Why are nanotechnologists still tinkering with the atom when the atom is not the underlying root of technology? Why is the pull of matter so strong, its allure so magnificent, and the temptation to pursue the path of intelligence so magnetic?

My teacher's response to these vital questions is found in an event that took place some 3400 years ago. It involved the first person in the history of civilization ever to truly apply nanotechnology.

THE FIRST
NANOTECHNOLOGY
SYMPOSIUM

"And he received the gold from their hand, and he fashioned it, with an engraving tool, and made a molten calf."
—Exodus 32:4

Some 3400 years ago we meet the very first nanotechnologist. His name was Moses, and he put together the first nanotechnology symposium in the famous biblical locale known as Mount Sinai. According to the *Zohar*, the story of Moses and the Revelation event is perhaps the most corrupted and misconstrued story of all time. Traditional organized religion tells us that Moses received ten Commandments inscribed on two stone tablets. The revelation of these Commandments took place when Moses was high up on Mount Sinai, and the Israelites were camped out at the base of the mountain.

We're told that while Moses was up on the mountain, the Israelites became impatient while awaiting his return, and began engaging in all of kinds of indulgent behavior, including sexual debauchery. Their impatience and doubt led them to build a Golden Calf to worship, in place of the one true God. After receiving the stone tablets, Moses returned. He saw the Golden Calf and all the decadent behavior that was taking place. In his anger,

Moses smashed the tablets and they shattered into pieces, thus bringing the Revelation event to a tragic conclusion.

The *Zohar*, universally acknowledged as the most authoritative wisdom of Kabbalah, states rather bluntly that anyone who reads this story literally is nothing short of a fool. Initially this statement might sound rather offensive, but the *Zohar* goes on to explain that the entire story of Moses and Mount Sinai is, in fact, an encoded message.

Decrypting the Sinai Code

According to the *Zohar*, the beneficent Force known as the Light of the Creator never commands or punishes. What is more, the very concept of Ten Commandments is a fraudulent interpretation of what the tablets were all about. This deception has led to intolerance, conflict, and bloodshed amongst the very people who were supposed to uphold these so-called Commandments.

My teacher told me, in no uncertain terms, that the so-called Ten Commandments have nothing to do with laws, obligations, Divine directives, or, least of all, Commandments. Rather, my teacher revealed that the number ten is a reference to the ten dimensions that compose true, timeless reality. Imagine the shock and bewilderment of people living hundreds of years ago, or thousands of years ago, upon learning that there are ten dimensions of reality. The whole idea of *other dimensions* only became part of the consciousness of modern physics in the 20th century. Yet Kabbalist Rav Shimon bar Yohai spoke of the ten-dimensional Universe to his companions over 2000 years ago, during a midnight study session in a cave in the region of Galilee.

This, however, was not what shook me to the core—I will get to that shortly. The *Zohar* tells us that Moses, utilizing the science and technology of Kabbalah, connected and bonded our physical dimension with the remaining nine other dimensions. These hidden, unobservable nine dimensions make up the *Tree of Life Reality*, the source of all wisdom and fulfillment that we have been discussing throughout this book.

These nine dimensions, which are imperceptible to the five senses, overflow with Divine Energy, infinite knowledge, joy, or in one word—Light. But what does a connection to this hidden reality mean in practical terms? What does it mean that Moses bonded our world to the *Tree of Life Reality?*

The Demise of Darkness

I must admit that when my teacher first taught me the truth about the Sinai/Revelation event, I was taken aback. I was shocked and flabbergasted. Essentially, the whole Sinai story comes down to one idea—*immortality!* There were no so-called Commandments. No handing down of a religion. No birth of a Judaic tradition. The Revelation on Mount Sinai ignited and discharged the full measure of the Light Force of God from the Endless World through nine dimensions into this tenth dimension that is our Universe.

When Moses bonded this physical world to the spiritual reality known as the *Tree of Life*, the infusion of Light and Energy was so powerful, it literally eradicated all darkness and death from the landscape of civilization. Immortality is what Sinai was all about. What I didn't understand at first was that this immortality was not limited to the human body, as we shall now discover.

Defining Death

When we become bored with life, it means our happiness has died; death has snuffed out a particular ray of Light known as *happiness*. When money problems strike, it means death has killed off our prosperity; our source of sustenance has died. When any form of chaos afflicts us, it means *order* has died. The so-called Angel of Death (or Angel of Space) is the sole culprit behind all of our unhappiness in every conceivable area of human activity. Whatever goes wrong in this world, or in our lives, the cause is always the same: somehow the death force infiltrated it.

Declining sales is not the cause of financial trouble in a business. Rather, the death force has impregnated the business, which is why sales have dropped and profits have disappeared. Order gives way to chaos because there is an opening, a fracture some-where in one's life, and the force of death, as concealed as dark-ness at night, stands ready to infiltrate that opening and wreak havoc and destruction.

Space is Death

Earlier we came to understand that there really is no Angel of Death but, rather, an Angel of Space; this means that when our happiness dies, we have actually disconnected ourselves from the source of all happiness—the *Tree of Life Reality*. There is space between us and this transcendent sublime realm. Any time chaos strikes, it's a direct consequence of having disconnected. We have created a space between ourselves and the hidden dimensions that flow with Light and abound with absolute joy. Space causes death in every area of our life.

Defining Immortality

Immortality, according to Kabbalah, not only includes the end of biological death but it also includes the presence of unending joy, wisdom, happiness, excitement, passion, and fulfillment beyond what our rational minds can possibly conceive. This is what Sinai was all about; this is what Moses achieved. Immortality! Not just for the Israelites, but for all mankind. It included within it the fulfillment of every conceivable desire a man and woman could possibly have—and more! Immortality refers to a rapturous level of happiness that never leaves, never dies.

Boredom, loneliness, sickness, anxiety, fear, and worry no longer exist for they are only the byproducts of death.

From the kabbalistic viewpoint, when you get to the essence of what all human beings want from life, it is *immortality* in all of its infinite manifestations.

THE DEATH OF IMMORTALITY

I asked my teacher and master what happened? Where did this energy called immortality go? Why is death still the predominant feature of our world?

Moses, the master told me, connected the world to the *Tree of Life Reality* by completely removing his ego from his nature.

Moses personally accomplished the task of resisting the final 1 Percent of ego. Moses attained a form similar to the Light; he shared and gave unconditionally, and through the Law of Attraction (*like attracts like*) Moses aligned and bonded all ten dimensions into one unified whole. Thus, on his merit alone, the entire world achieved oneness with the *Tree of Life Reality*. But this condition would not last.

As we learned at the outset of this chapter, the realm of the *Tree of Life* can only be accessed through consciousness, specifically through the elevation of consciousness by eradicating the ego and selfishness. Moses achieved this. Moses bonded with the Light Force that permeated the *Tree of Life Reality* because he was selfless. He was not pious. He was not a deeply religious man. He was selfless. Ego—the Adversary—was banished from his very essence. Moses' power was the result of purification, of cleansing his consciousness of the negative *Desire to Receive for the Self Alone*, and replacing it with a consciousness of sharing that put the needs of others first, unconditionally, with genuine humility.

Moses did not eradicate 99 Percent of his ego, nor love others with 99 Percent of his heart and soul; if he had, the bond between the physical and metaphysical world of Light would never have taken place. Moses was all about *100 Percent*. Moses went all the way, which earned him the right to hold the "Tablets of Immortality."

What Went Wrong

Unfortunately, the Israelites were not of the same consciousness. Theirs was a "What's in it for me?" mindset. Their consciousness created space. The story of the Israelites building a Golden Calf is actually code for using one's ego, intellect, and a *physical inter-mediary* as the interface between this world and the *Tree of Life Reality*.

The concept of a *Golden Calf* is the code that conceals a deeper truth: that the Israelites were not yet ready to receive the full complement of the Light Force of the Creator; their transformation of consciousness had not taken place. Instead they surrendered control to an *idol*, to the realm of physicality, to the realm of space. They were incomplete in their resistance to the influence of the Adversary.

What this all comes down to is that they did not want to give up the ego and choose unconditional love for their neighbor.

The Light Was Lost

As a result, the power of immortality was lost. The bond was broken and a separation had taken place. This is the meaning of the breaking of the Tablets. The Tablets and their "Ten Commandments" signify the bonding of all ten dimensions into one complete whole, the 99 Percent and the 1 Percent. The shattering of the Tablets concerns the *space* that is created when a bond is broken, when disconnection takes place.

Death was reborn along with that space.

Perhaps Another Day

In a cave near the top of Mount Sinai, a second set of Tablets was then created by Moses. This second set of Tablets, according to the *Zohar*, contains the wisdom, technology, and raw power of Kabbalah, as well as that of the *Zohar*.

The ancient kabbalists tell us that both the shattered pieces of the immortality Tablets and the second set of Tablets were put inside the Ark of the Covenant, which means that the possibility of repairing the broken tablets and removing the space that separates us from the *Tree of Life Reality* is also present in the Ark. The Ark contains both the problem and the cure. Here we discover the underlying reason the world has been held spellbound for millennia by the search for the Ark of the Covenant. On a subconscious soul-level, we all know what the contents of the Ark offer humanity—a chance to repair what is broken, to remove the space between our atoms and between people, as well as the distance between this physical reality and the realm of Divine energy and Light.

My teacher told me that there would be a new window of opportunity to re-establish the forces of immortality in the world once again, to restore the Light and Energy Force that was lost on Sinai. The teachings of Kabbalah would be made available to the entire world and, when it came, this time would be unmistakable. Evidently we have arrived at that extraordinary moment in history, thanks to my teacher Rav Brandwein, and his teacher Rav Ashlag, who opened the doors of Kabbalah to lay people for the first time in human history. However, that initial opening was limited to a select few within the Holy Land. My teacher —and his teacher— had something more ambitious in mind.

The Response that Shocked Me to the Core

At this point in my studies my teacher revealed to me an insight that shook me to the foundations of my soul. The master told me that I would have to be the one to disseminate the once-forbidden *Zohar* and the secrets of immortality to the world for the first time in human history. In a million years I would never have dreamed that the ancient vaults of kabbalistic wisdom, which had been sealed shut for two thousand years, would open up on my watch.

My teacher told me that I would undoubtedly face unimaginable pressure and pain from those who fought long and hard throughout the centuries to keep Kabbalah secret. He was right, which is why it has taken close to forty years to produce the book you are reading. My path to this moment in time, although filled with more aches than I am able to convey by written word alone, is one that I would beg the Creator to allow me to do all over again. For the difficulties of my path pale in comparison to the immeasurable fulfillment I have experienced. One hour with my teacher would have made ten lifetimes of pain worthwhile.

Many situations and memories immediately come to mind but I would be remiss if I did not speak of the one that brought the most pain to my family—to Karen, my wife, partner, friend, and soul mate, and to my two sons, Yehuda and Michael. Is it ironic that I, who have been called a kabbalist by my beloved teacher and by my devoted students, whose assignment was to share an ancient source of wisdom and power that would alleviate all suffering, including the scourge of death itself, should myself experience what the medical community diagnosed as a stroke? In fact, it is not ironic at all. Perhaps only those whose lineage includes kabbalists, those entrusted with Kabbalah's ancient secrets, could possibly understand that. But it is akin to the idea that, to win a heavyweight championship bout, both the challenger and the champion must step into the ring.

I have often wondered if this was the reason that, for 4000 years, Kabbalah was limited to a select and privileged few—those prepared to step into the ring. Could this be why so many who were exposed to this path throughout the ages simply walked away when the waters got rough?

My teacher taught me a lesson that had been taught to him by his teacher: one can only share that which he himself possesses. Having suffered this stroke and managed to continue working on this book from another level of consciousness—much to the consternation of medical science, the worlds leading hospitals and universities—I can now share with others what it means to resist the Adversary even when the going gets tough. And so the work continues.

Nevertheless, a moment never passes by when I don't appreciate the fact that I had the merit and good fortune to be on watch during this historic period— though I admit, I don't understand why this is.

The Last Step

Admittedly, my shock at the responsibility that was thrust upon me by my teacher would never have subsided if not for the strength, courage, and determination of Karen, my soul mate, who made the daring and historic decision to allow all men, women, and children—Israelites, Muslims, Christians, Buddhists, and atheists alike—to study from the *Zohar* and draw from its bottomless well of wisdom. When Karen first came to this conclusion I knew, without question, that our lives would be in danger, and in constant turmoil. I must confess, without Karen, my plan would have been to limit the study of Kabbalah to those already steeped in biblical wisdom. My beloved teacher and master, however, foresaw the presence of Karen in my life. He left this world before Karen and I were married, but a true kabbalist is never limited or governed by Cause and Effect, or by time and space. My teacher remains with me to this very day, not just in memory, but in a tangible way that I pray the rest of the world will finally come to understand is absolutely possible.

I am blessed beyond all measure to be able to share this wisdom with the world and take an active part, along with my soul mate, in what will now be the dawn of immortality. Before us lies an opportunity for the final revelation of Light and Divine energy that will return our world to a permanent state of immortality and unending happiness. However, the *Zohar* cautions us that the opportunity to repeat the same mistakes we made on Mount Sinai will be ever-present during this time. The Adversary will have one last crack at us. In this next section it is my intent to lay out the formula for achieving immortality through an authentic nanotechnology method while, at the same time, identifying the dangerous pitfalls and traps that loom on the horizon.

PART EIGHT:

THE PATH TO THE ONCE UNTHINKABLE!

TWO PATHS TO HAPPILY EVER AFTER

Mankind possesses the God-given option of choosing one of two paths to arrive at immortality:

1. The Path of Suffering;
2. The Path of Kabbalistic Nanotechnology.

When we bleed and suffer in war, or in a divorce, or in business, or because of poor health, this suffering removes a layer of ego. The pain cleanses some reactive consciousness from our nature. Eventually, over the course of many lifetimes, we will suffer enough so that finally the ego will be banished from our landscape. When all traces of the ego have departed, the sharing gene of God sparks to life, and now we are able to *Receive for the Sake of Sharing*. We will achieve immortality.

On Mount Sinai, the Divine Force that humankind designates as God gave Moses an alternative path to the same goal that could prevent the body and soul from suffering along the way. This path was kabbalistic nanotechnology. (Not surprisingly, the great thinkers of history, from Sir Isaac Newton to Wilhelm Leibniz, from Plato to Pythagoras, all concurred that it was Kabbalah that Moses received on Sinai, not the basis for any organized religion.) On this extraordinary path, it is only the ego that experiences suffering. It is only the ego that is required to experience any form of pain. And ultimately it is only the ego that will have to experience death. This is, without question, a more pleasant way to achieve our destiny than the path of suffering.

However, the Adversary will always be there to direct you onto the path of bodily and soul suffering. The Adversary will tell you that Moses received a religion on Mount Sinai, not a technology. Or the Adversary will tell you *how* the physical laws of the world work, but not *why* things are as they are, thereby limiting you to only being able to treat the symptoms, and never the Cause.

Fortunately, free will gives you the ability to reject the Adversary.

The Thought of Creation

From God's perspective, the outcome of traveling both these paths is a foregone conclusion. It is God's desire to share unending happiness with the Vessel, the souls of humanity, eternally. Life is that simple. Getting there is a bit more complicated. Nonetheless, everything that takes place in the Universe, from a pebble rolling down a mountain somewhere in New Zealand to the social and economic upheavals that ripple across continents, from the movements of the ocean tides to the laws of particle physics, everything, at every moment, is moving toward this ultimate goal.

We are going to be happy and immortal, whether we believe it or not. All of humankind will participate in redemption and endless fulfillment, including atheists and skeptics. Our free choice only determines how we reach that ultimate destination. An individual can choose to take the easy, scenic route or the painful, turbulent path. The Universe is indifferent, because a happy outcome is guaranteed either way; it's up to us to decide which path to trek. It's in our hands, and it has been since the Sinai Event 3400 years ago.

Let us now examine the two routes to immortality in more detail.

KABBALAH VERSUS SCIENCE

Renowned scientist, author, and inventor Ray Kurzweil was presented the National Medal of Technology Award at the White House by President Bill Clinton. Called "a modern day Edison," Kurzweil was inducted into the Inventor's Hall of Fame in 2002. According to Kurzweil, we are about twenty years away from achieving immortality through nanotechnology. He foresees three bridges that need to be crossed in order to reach this goal. Kurzweil puts it this way:

> Bridge One has to do with taking full advantage of today's knowledge of biology in order to dramatically slow down aging and disease processes. This will enable us to stay in as good a shape as possible for when Bridge Two technologies become available. Bridge Two is the biotechnology revolution, which will give us the tools to reprogram our biology and the biochemical information processes underlying our biology. We're in the early stages of

*that revolution already, but in fifteen years we will
have, to a large extent, mastery over our biology.
That will take us to the Third Bridge, the nanotechnology revolution, where we can rebuild our bodies
and brains at the molecular level. This will enable
us to fix the remaining problems that are difficult to
address within the confines of biology and ultimately allow us to go beyond the limitations of biology
altogether. So the idea is to get on Bridge One now,
so we can be alive and healthy when the biotechnology and nanotechnology revolutions come to fruition.
Our aim is to live long enough to live forever.*

In *Enlightenment Magazine*, an article and interview entitled,
*Chasing Immortality, An interview with Ray Kurzweil by Craig
Hamilton,* Kurzweil foresees nano-bots the size of blood cells,
teeming throughout the human body repairing arteries, brain
cells, bones, and muscles. These microscopic robots will destroy
diseases and rebuild our organs. He foresees downloading DNA
modifications from the Internet. Kurzweil even sees a day when
human beings will not need a heart to live.

Does Kurzweil sound like a crackpot? Along with his impressive
credentials, Kurzweil's ability to spot scientific trends is well
established. In his first book, "The Age of Intelligent Machines,"
published way back in 1990, Kurzweil predicted that a global
computer network would emerge in the very near future. It took
some three years for the World Wide Web and the Internet to
transform our world and confirm his forecast. Kurzweil also predicted that a computer would defeat a chess champion by 1999.

The year was 1997 when chess master Garry Kasparov lost a match to an IBM supercomputer named Deep Blue.

One then might wonder: Why do we need Kabbalah if we have Kurzweil? If science is going to perform the trick of immortality, why bother with an ancient technology that stresses human behavior over intelligent machines and microscopic robots that do it all for us?

In other words, if I can use Nanorobots to build giant-screen TVs, DVD players, sports cars, and swimming pools, and I can program these robots to manufacture food for famine-stricken communities throughout the world, as well as rebuild all the organs of the human body, why do we need Kabbalah? What is the difference between science's nanotechnology and kabbalistic nanotechnology?

The answer is two-fold. The first part of the answer is found in a 4000 year-old kabbalistic concept known as the *Four Phases*.

THE FOUR PHASES

The Four Phases, according to ancient kabbalists, operate at every level of existence. There is nothing in our world that does not undergo these Four Phases before manifesting in a physical form.

The Four Phases are as follows:

- **PHASE ONE:** *The potential of the potential*
- **PHASE TWO:** *The actualization of the potential*
- **PHASE THREE:** *The potential of the actualization*
- **PHASE FOUR:** *The actualization of the actualization*

For an example of how the Four Phases work, let's turn to the task of constructing a building.

Construction of a Building

- **PHASE ONE:** *The potential of the potential*

   A developer decides to build an office tower in Manhattan. Although he *sees* the building completed in his mind, it only exists in consciousness, in the non-physical state of pure thought. This is the level of pure potential.

- **PHASE TWO:** *The actualization of the potential*

   The developer begins to initiate and develop his original concept. He hires an architect to draw up blueprints. The information in the blueprints still represents the consciousness, or thought-level phase of the building. However, the thought is evolving. Its potential is being expressed and *actualized* on paper. The thought now exists in two dimensions—in consciousness and on the physical blueprint.

- **PHASE THREE:** *The potential of the actualization*

   Once the blueprints are complete, all the physical raw materials for constructing the building are purchased and delivered to the construction site. This includes steel beams, concrete, wiring, plumbing, drywall, bricks, glass windows, etc. All of these physical elements will appear in the final actualization of the building. The concept of a completed building is now in a state of *physical* potential, as opposed to *thought* potential.

- **PHASE FOUR: *The actualization of the actualization***
  The building is completed. The developer calls a press conference and shows off the finished high-rise office tower to the world.

Everything in our physical world goes through these Four Phases. This includes the creation of a flourishing business, or a successful marriage, or a blockbuster Hollywood motion picture. The Four Phases are also evident in the bankruptcy of a business, the demise of a marriage, and the creation of a Hollywood motion picture flop.

An obvious question now arises: *What determines whether Phase Four is a success, a failure, or somewhere in between?* The answer to this question lies in Phase One.

THE POWER OF PHASE ONE

Because Phase One contains *both* the original germ of a thought *and* its final manifestation, this phase contains all the other phases, namely, Phases Two, Three, and Four, within it! The developer's original thought was not the creation of a blueprint in Phase Two. Nor was it the tons of concrete and miles of wiring and plumbing found in Phase Three. The developer's initial thought was an image of a completed building filled with high-profile tenants paying rental rates for office space. This leads to a fundamental principle of Kabbalah:

- **The End is Always Contained in the Beginning**

Or

- **The Cause Always Contains the Effect**

The Cause of the building was the developer's initial thought. Likewise, the Effect—the completed building—was *also* originally present in the developer's consciousness. When we observe the workings of nature we can begin to comprehend this kabbalistic concept: an apple seed contains the root, trunk, branches, and final fruit of the complete apple tree.

One might ask why this principle is so important. There are two critically important reasons why this process should be understood:

1. **Phase One determines whether Phase Four will be a huge success or a spectacular failure.**

2. **In order for kabbalistic nanotechnology to work, we must access Phase One if we are to change the subsequent phases and deliver a new outcome in Phase Four.**

If a gardener plants a defective apple seed, an unhealthy apple tree is the inevitable result. This is simple Cause and Effect. If the gardener plants a healthy apple seed, one can expect a healthy apple tree to emerge. The student of Kabbalah, the practitioner of kabbalistic nanotechnology, must always keep in mind that Phase One determines success or failure. Everything else that emerges in the subsequent phases is merely the effect of the initial Phase One seed.

The Secret of Phase One

If one alters the branch of a tree, one affects only the branch. But if one modifies a seed, one affects the root, trunk, branch, leaf, and final fruit! That is the ultimate in control. It's the only way to affect genuine change in our world and in our lives. And in the view of the *Zohar*, the ultimate seed level—Phase One—is never found in the world of physicality. Everything physical first begins in the state known as *consciousness*. Phase One is pure consciousness.

Before the Wright Brothers invented and produced the first airplane, it existed as a thought. Before N. J. Conte invented the pencil in 1795, it existed as an idea inside Conte's head. The same holds true for William Carrier; he built the first air conditioner in 1902, but the idea first originated in his mind as a concept. Kellogg's Corn Flakes® did not magically appear in a bowl of milk. The idea for this brand of cereal initially existed as an inspiration inside William Kellogg's head in 1906. Arthur Wynne of Liverpool first had to dream up the idea of a crossword puzzle before his invention could appear in a physical newspaper on December 21, 1913.

Consciousness is *always* the seed and the Cause behind all physical manifestations. Any physical appearance is merely the Effect. Everything begins with consciousness, in the realm of the immaterial. This truth is right in front of our noses, yet we are blind to it.

The Crux of the Matter

Here lies the critical limitation of science's version of nanotechnology. Scientific nanotechnology does not address Phase One. By contrast, as we have learned throughout this book, Kabbalah shows us that the atom itself is composed of consciousness. As we've repeated throughout this book, desire and the electrons in our body are one and the same. They are simply two different names for a single force. The subatomic particle we call an electron is merely *receiving consciousness* in physical form. Think of it as "frozen consciousness."

Science's version of Nanorobots that are capable of tinkering are tinkering with the electron in Phase Two, or with the atom in Phase Three. But if you tinker with the non-physical consciousness that is the *Cause* behind the electron, now you have established control over the entire physical realm, and can thus determine the Effects that manifest in our physical reality.

The Phase One Problem

As we have discussed, 99 Percent of the time our actions are rooted in ego and reactive behavior. We are unaware that an Adversary even exists. We believe the influences of the Adversary are our own thoughts. We take ownership of these thoughts and desires because we are not aware of the ego's independent presence in our life.

Thus it is that all of our activities are motivated by self-interest. Sometimes this is blatantly obvious, but most of the time it is deceptively subtle. In this way every action we perform, every venture we begin, whether in a personal relationship or a business, becomes rooted in ego and self-interest. Ego infuses Phase One. And ego does not produce Light, but rather separation. Thus, somewhere down the line, in Phases Two, Three, or Four, failure or chaos will materialize in our life.

Sickness and Disease: Space as the Culprit, and Consciousness as the Cause

Sickness in a body, or sickness in a business or personal relationship, is caused by consciousness—and nothing else—according to the *Zohar*. This is Phase One. It was negative, selfish consciousness that created cigarettes, nuclear radiation, and toxic waste. And it's negative consciousness that weakens our immune systems and makes us vulnerable to external sources of negativity.

If we merely treat Phase Two, Three, and Four, we displace the problem—we do not, in any way, remedy it. We are displacing the problem by having failed to cut out its root. We have instituted a coping mechanism, but we have not cured our world of the diseases that bring so much pain into our lives.

THE PROMISE OF KABBALISTIC NANO

The wonders of nanotechnology will be accomplished through the power of our thoughts. When our consciousness is completely free of the Adversary, when we have completely eradicated self-ishness from our being, our thoughts and consciousness will freely penetrate and motivate matter. Our consciousness will interact and communicate instantaneously with every atom in every object. We will stop decay with the power of our thoughts, because thought is the ultimate source of reality. We will remove the space between the atoms in our bodies, and ensure that they hold hands forever.

Our thoughts will repair our kidneys. Our thoughts will regenerate our hearts. Our thoughts will unleash the full power of our brains. We will have the ability to use our thoughts to gather atoms into molecules in the air and form them into food, cars, or anything else we desire, because these are only frozen forms of con-sciousness. However, this power to manifest thoughts in physical form will only materialize when the Adversary is 100 Percent removed from our consciousness, and not before.

When our thoughts and consciousness are truly only interested in serving our neighbor and fulfilling their needs, this power will be unleashed within us.

Love Thy Neighbor is the one prerequisite to allowing the God Gene, the "God" consciousness to blossom within us.

THE ULTIMATE
SAFTEY VALVE

We will never have to worry about people abusing the unlimited power of kabbalistic nanotechnology to create weapons of mass destruction. People will never misuse this power to receive personal material wealth and domination over others, because the full power of human consciousness will only be unleashed when every trace of selfishness and reactive nature is eradicated from our being. This dramatic shift in human consciousness needs to take place first. This is the only reason mankind has not discovered this power thus far.

We will only develop the power of mind over matter and kabbalistic nanotechnology in direct proportion to the amount of transformation that we make in our lives. As I said at the very outset of this book, when the Vessel in this world removes every ounce of selfishness, every trace of ego from its nature, the God Gene sparks to life. At that moment we will understand, appreciate, value, and recognize the limitless joy and power that true sharing engenders. Then we will offer love and friendship without conditions because we will know (not believe) that it gives us total control over every electron, proton, and neutron in our bodies, and in the Universe. When the body (*Desire to Receive*) is in a constant state of sharing, the atoms that form the body will establish a constant state of bonding by sharing their electrons. Atoms will forever remain bonded together, continuing a dance that will never end; the dance of sharing electrons will give rise to the endless dance of life.

Unfortunately, most of the world has no idea that this transformation is the purpose of life; 99 Percent of the world is not aware that learning how to share and care for one another by triumphing over our own self-interest and ego is the very reason for our existence. The world has failed, thus far, to realize that unconditional love and kind behavior towards others unleash the awesome power of consciousness and kabbalistic nanotechnology. And perhaps most astonishingly, we have failed to grasp the idea that *Enlightened Greed* must be the sole motivator behind our acts of tolerance and human dignity.

The Weapon of Time

Cunningly, the Adversary has tripped us up over the centuries, keeping us in the dark about these extraordinary truths. The Adversary cleverly attached the idea of morals, ethics, and organized religion to sharing behavior. And what did we see? We saw corrupt people profiting and honest people failing. But that too was a trick. The Adversary merely used the concept of *time* to create the illusion that good behavior does not pay. Time separates Cause from Effect. Time creates distance between a crime and its consequence. Time produces a delay between resistance and its reward, hoodwinking us into believing that egocentricity leads to success and that kindness is a dead-end street.

CONNECTING
THE DOTS

The Adversary has thought out his entire game plan quite well. He has blinded us to the inner workings of life. In other words, when we react, we do not see the immediate repercussions of our actions. Instead, our ego receives a pleasurable infusion of energy, handed to us by the Adversary. Or we acquire some material reward.

This is how the clever Adversary blinds us to the fact that there is negative karma headed our way as a result of our reactive behavior, which has created more separation between the Light and ourselves. Unfortunately, we do not detect this added darkness immediately, because the Adversary gives us some temporary Light to throw us off balance. He uses time to delay the arrival of darkness. It may take a few months, or many years, but after we behave reactively, darkness and chaos will inevitably arrive at our doorstep in some form. When that moment makes its appearance, most people will never be able to connect the dots and make the connection between the sudden arrival of chaos and their own previous egocentric behavior.

Accordingly, we mistakenly believe that life is shaped by random forces, such as chaos or blind luck. We think existence is all about cycles and compromising on what life can offer us. Some years we experience good fortune. Other years the cycle shifts and we undergo turmoil and strife. We believe that's just how life is, so we engage in even more self-indulgent living to compensate for the chaos in the other areas of our life. Life becomes a vicious cycle from which there is no escape.

When our chaos becomes serious enough, we try to fix our lives. Unfortunately, we have been conditioned to fiddle with Phases Two, Three, and Four. We wind up blaming others for circumstances "beyond our control," seeing ourselves as helpless victims simply because we fail to realize that our own Phase One consciousness is the fundamental cause of all our misfortune.

My teacher always told me that the most difficult thing to do is to take responsibility for our own chaos. The Adversary will always have you pointing the finger at everyone and everything—*except at your own self.*

A green activist and a polluter *both* operate from the same inherent reactive consciousness. The fact that one has good intentions and the other does not has nothing to do with it. As the saying goes—*The road to hell is paved with good intentions.* When one or both can admit that the Adversary exists, they will have passed the test of true consciousness. If they commit to working on removing the Adversary from their nature, eradicating self-interest and ego from all of their actions along the way, then they are changing the world by virtue of changing themselves.

THE MAGIC BULLET

Science dreams about a magic bullet that can specifically target a cancer cell without harming the rest of the cells in the body. Kabbalah already has the magic bullet. It's called **accountability!** When we take responsibility for every bit of chaos in our life, we recognize that our own consciousness is the cause of our misfortune, or ultimately our fortune, it is up to us. Once we have this accountability consciousness, instead of having to suffer emotionally or physically, we are operating in Phase One.

The more accountable we are, and the more laser-focused we are on the target, the greater chances we have for a genuine healing. But of course all of this is easier said than done. The Adversary will tell you that the key to the life you lead is the food you eat, or the air you breathe, or it's hereditary. He will provide you with 101 reasons why it cannot be as simple as your own consciousness. *That is just too easy, too simplistic; it's impractical, naive, irresponsible thinking.*

Of course, it's tempting to buy into that argument, as it shrewdly absolves us of all responsibility. That victim consciousness gets us off the hook. Being a victim is so much easier as we get to retain our egos.

The Fallacy of Positive Thinking

Do not be deceived by the popular and compelling notion of positive thoughts and the power of positive thinking when we talk about the role of consciousness in creating and controlling our reality. It's not negative thoughts that cause our problems. *It's selfish thoughts.* You can have positive thoughts all day long about all the wonderful things you want to receive from life. But that is just as dangerous. Why? You are in a *receiving* mode. *It's all about me!*

Thinking positively about fulfilling our own self-seeking desires represents the dark side of the Law of Attraction. If we direct our positive thoughts at *Receiving for the Self Alone*, we will receive material items, but their source will be the Adversary, for we will have attained similarity of form with him. At the same time, this consciousness creates space from the true Source of happiness—the Light of the Creator—for we are now in opposition to the positive Force of sharing. We are receiving. Inevitably, sooner or later, chaos will return to the scene.

The Law of Attraction can be used for our own ends, or it can be used for the sole purpose of serving the needs and desires of our neighbor. One approach leads to death, the other to immortality. One approach is governed by senseless greed, the other by *Enlightened Greed*.

The Bonds of Sharing

When a problem confronts you, and your thought is, "What pain did I cause another individual that caused my problem to become manifest in the first place?" you have arrived at Phase One. You have found the elusive immaterial Cause level of all physical causes. Likewise, when you say, "I want to remove the pain that I caused the other person, in order to receive more Light in my own life," you are utilizing *Enlightened Greed for the Soul*. You are putting the needs of the other person ahead of your own. Kabbalah says you can have anything, and you can ask for anything from the Creator, provided you put the welfare of the other person ahead of your own.

When you focus on eliminating your own negative traits, the technology of Kabbalah is fully activated. It's running on all cylinders, operating at maximum capacity, correcting the consciousness and removing the egocentric traits that caused you to be greedy for the ego in the first place. Once that aspect of your consciousness is corrected, the problem must dissolve and disappear. It must, and it will.

THE POWER OF REMOVING SPACE

Space is the sole problem, according the doctrines of the *Zohar*. When I saw the power of my teacher, and his ability to remove all space between him and his Arab friend by offering this man unconditional kindness, little did I realize that this act of loving was the most profound technology available to humankind. Yet it remains the most difficult to understand and apply.

THE ULTIMATE POWER OF LOVE THY NEIGHBOR

A COVALENT BOND:
THE APPLE THIEF AND THE SHOPKEEPER

There was a once a King who ruled his Kingdom with an iron fist. And he had good reason. The vast numbers of his subjects were scoundrels. It was a dog-eat-dog existence, where each man was out for himself.

One day, a man by the name of Nathanial was caught stealing an apple. Nathanial was not really a bad person. It wasn't his nature to steal from anyone. But after living among so many villains for so many years, he simply gave in to his selfish instinct on this one occasion. Unfortunately, it was a bad time to make his first mistake.

The King decided to make an example of poor Nathanial to send a message to the rest of the people.

Nathanial was given a sentence of death by the King. He accepted his fate without any fuss. After all, he had no one to blame but himself.

The King asked Nathanial if he had any last request. He did. Nathanial asked if he could have three days to settle various affairs in his life. Nathanial had to pay off some debts, he owed a few personal favors, and he wanted to say goodbye to all of his loved ones. He figured he could tidy it all up in three days.

The King, impressed by Nathanial's simple accept-ance of his fate and by his sense of responsibility, wanted to accommodate this last request. But there was an obvious problem. "If I grant you this temporary reprieve," the King said, "I have no assurances that you will ever return to fulfill your sentence."

Nathanial understood the King's dilemma. "I have an idea," Nathanial responded. "Suppose I arrange for a good friend to stand in for me until I return. If I am late, you can execute my friend in my place." The King laughed. "If you can find someone who will take your place, I will grant you your three days. But if you are even one minute late, you can be sure your friend will be hung on the gallows."

Nathanial asked his best friend, a shopkeeper by the name of Simon, to stand in his place. Simon had known Nathanial since they were young chil-dren. He loved him like a brother and respected his friend dearly. Simon said he would be honored to go into temporary custody for Nathanial.

Simon was handcuffed and detained while Nathanial hurried off to wind up his affairs. "Remember," the King yelled out, "One minute late and I will hang your best friend."

One day passed…then two more, and Nathanial did not return. The King ordered Simon to the gallows and the hangman's noose was slipped around Simon's neck. The hangman tightened it. A hood was put over Simon's head.

And then, suddenly, a voice was heard screaming far off in the distance. "Stop! Stop! I have returned!" It was Nathanial. "Please, I beg you," Nathanial cried to the King. "Remove the noose from my best friend. This is my fate, not his."

But the King replied, "You are an hour late."

Nathanial was so out of breath he could hardly talk. "Let me explain, your Majesty. My horse became lame. I was forced to run all the way back. That is why I am late. It is I who should die. Not my dear friend."

Simon then began to cry out. The hangman removed the hood from his head. "That is not true. I am the one who should die today. We had an agreement. Besides, I could not stand here and watch you, my best friend, die before my eyes. Nor could I bear living without you. You were late. So it will be I who will die today."

Nathanial's eyes welled up with tears. "I beg you, your majesty. Do not listen to him. Do not let my best friend die. It is I who was originally sentenced to death, not Simon. If you kill him I will not be able to live with the pain of seeing my dear friend depart from this Earth. I beg you to take me."

Simon and Nathanial continued arguing back and forth about who would die that day. Not surprisingly, the King was taken aback. In a land rampant with hooligans, the King was not accustomed to seeing such acts of unconditional friendship. Nevertheless, a decision had to be made. The King might be a strict ruler, but he was a fair ruler, and justice had to be meted out according to the law of the land.

"I have reached a final verdict," the King said. "Today neither one of you shall die. For I realize that no matter which one of you dies today, I will still be killing two men. The original sentence called for only one man to die. Thus, I am forced to set you both free."

The secret encoded inside this ancient kabbalistic tale reveals why one should love his neighbor, why an individual should put the interests of another ahead of his own: *Enlightened Self-Interest!* Based upon the law of the land, Nathanial was destined to die. But when he was late returning, Simon, his best friend, now found himself on the gallows. Both men warranted death sentences, but both men avoided their fates by letting go of *all* selfish inclinations. There was not a trace of self-interest within their hearts. They rejected selfishness and considered only the welfare of the other person, unconditionally, with no strings attached. Both men offered their own bodies (the electron) on behalf of the other and thus, like a covalent bond, the two men became as one. Seeing this, the King realized he could not kill one without killing the other.

Both friends had removed any potential space that might exist between them.

Overturning Death

This kabbalistic parable tells us something quite extraordinary: we can defy the laws of the land, including the laws of physics, and even the fate of death, if we share love unconditionally, removing any space that might exist between ourselves and others. Genuinely putting the welfare of others ahead of our own serves our own interests.

THE ILLUSION

Our Adversary has but one function: to convince us that the above story is a nice tale of morals and ethics that does not possess any technology that could be applied in our lives. And if you are completely honest with yourself, you will notice that doubts and fear and skepticism might very well be battling you at this very moment. The Adversary is such a brilliant and clever illusionist that we truly believe that we are helpless, and unable to control atoms with our consciousness.

Love Thy Neighbor was never meant to be a religious precept or commandment motivated by a religious code of ethics.

The seed of religion has obviously been corrupted, because time and time again the fruits of religion have been bloodshed, war, intolerance, and conflict between the peoples who populate this planet. More blood has been spilled in the name of religion than in any other cause in human history. I've often wondered how many times a person continues to bet on a losing horse before he finally wises up.

But now the Adversary responds and cries out telling us that religion offers us hope. This is true: we *hope* things will change, yet for some reason they do not. As a result we surrender our fate to a religious establishment that has failed for some 2000 years to eradicate pain and suffering from the human landscape. We are told that the Almighty works in mysterious ways, and when we cannot cure the mysterious ailments in our bodies, or our businesses, the *hope* offered by religion allows us to *cope* with our pain. But the kabbalists ask: Is this what life is really all about? Is coping, hoping, and waiting for relief—suffering all the while—part of the original intent of the Creator?

Therein lies the problem with the consciousness known as organized religion. It is founded on coping. It offers us hope, but not clear-cut solutions that deliver clear-cut results. If "*religious consciousness*" could deliver authentic miracles it would have delivered world peace long ago. Furthermore, a miracle shouldn't be a role of the dice so that sometimes we get a miracle and other times we don't. According to Kabbalah, no one can perform a miracle or a healing on your behalf. That ability is your God-given gift, and your responsibility. It is your inheritance and your destiny.

HOW TO INCREASE YOUR GREED

When you realize that behavior motivated by consciousness is the root cause of your problems and your good fortune, your greed for happiness will amplify. You will be motivated to engage in sharing behavior because you know it pays off. If it didn't, kabbalists would not work day and night uprooting their ego and sharing with others.

The following story can shed some Light on the Universal Laws of life, and why greed is the key to changing our behavior.

THE BOY WHO ROSE TO BE KING

There was once a great King whose wife was unable to bear him any children. Despite their unfortunate situation, the royal couple lived a good life. They ruled their Kingdom with great compassion, treating their subjects as members of their own family. As the King approached old age he knew it was time to prepare a worthy successor to his throne. Accordingly, he offered all the young boys of his kingdom a chance to become his adopted son for the purpose of inheriting the King's crown.

Hundreds of distinguished families in nearby villages enlisted their sons as potential candidates.

The King knew it was important for the boy to possess a special character and talent. So he devised a plan that would allow him to select the right person for adoption. The King gave all the boys identical flower seeds along with 6-inch terra cotta clay pots in which to grow miniature red roses. The boy who grew the most beautiful bouquet of roses would be the one chosen to become the future King.

There was one lad from a very poor family who entered the competition. His name was Ariel. This little ragamuffin had never learned to read or write because his family could not afford to send him to school. The young boy had to work all day in order to help his father feed the family. Ariel was actually excited about the royal competition, for now he would have an equal chance to achieve the greatest dream of all – the chance to become a real King.

Ariel gave it his best shot. He poured the finest soil into the pot. He added special nutrients. He watered the plant with the purest water he could find. And he bathed the plant in warm sunlight every day. Sadly, nothing happened. Ariel was distraught. His seeds had failed to sprout. Not a single stem popped out of the rich, black soil in his pot.

Ariel became even more upset when he visited other boys in the village. All of them had pots full of the most beautiful miniature red roses in full bloom. Ariel was heartbroken.

When the time to judge the winner came, the King summoned all the boys to his palace. All the potted plants were put out on public display in the Royal Gardens. Thousands of people gathered to see who would win the contest. Amid the sea of flaming red roses Ariel's empty pot stood out like a sore thumb, much to his embarrassment. The King carefully surveyed all the plants. He meticulously examined each stem, every branch and petal.

Suddenly, to the complete surprise of everyone— especially Ariel— the King selected the empty pot! As you might imagine, the other boys were shocked. And the crowd was stunned. Gasps and whispers flooded the Royal Gardens, but the King raised his hand to silence his subjects. Then he smiled and explained his reason for choosing the empty pot.

"I purposely gave all the boys defective flower seeds," the King admitted. "Not one of the seeds I had given out could grow a single petal. But I see that only one boy among you had the integrity and courage to tell the truth. This is the kind of valor that is required to rule a great Kingdom."

And so it was that Ariel and his family became adopted members of the royal family. To no one's surprise, Ariel grew up to become a worthy successor to a wise old King.

Life will offer endless temptations and opportunities to be unkind, deceitful, or self-centered. If, like Ariel, we resist these urges, we activate the power of nanotechnology. It is our consciousness that connects and controls the electrons, protons, and neutrons that form the atom. This is true mind over matter.

A LOSING BATTLE

Suppose your greed has now expanded to the point where you are committed to resisting your ego, and to embracing the technology known as *Love Thy Neighbor*. You've read this book and you accept the principles that it espouses. Why is it still difficult to perform the action of resistance? Why is the Adversary still such a powerful and dominating force in our lives?

Well, we may all know that following a healthy diet has a terrific impact on the way we feel each day. Yet, all too often we choose foods that contain only empty calories, foods that work against a healthy lifestyle. Sometimes the temptation is simply too strong, and we wind up succumbing to it.

Knowing with certainty that a technology works is simply not enough, there's still something missing. How do you muster the strength and willpower to defeat the Adversary? How do you gain access to the innermost depths of your being so you can battle the Adversary toe-to-toe on his home turf? Our enemy battles us at the level of consciousness. How do we take the battle there? Once again, nanotechnology provides a way to help us understand.

PART NINE:

ENTER
THE
ROBOTS

THE NANOROBOTS

Science understands the problem associated with gaining access to that innermost level of the material world—the world of atoms. Clearly, scientists cannot touch an atom or manipulate it with their hands or even the finest of instruments. Thus, they envision the creation of atom-sized Nanorobots that contain software programmed to direct and guide them to perform various functions.

Kabbalists revealed a Divine Alphabet, a sequence of 22 DNA-like letters that were created to assist all of humanity 4000 years ago. They included a technology called *The Names of God*. Of course God didn't really have various names. These are codes that transfer the consciousness of God to our physical world—just as a writer transfers his thoughts and ideas to another person by writing a book. These particular Names of God are like Nanorobots that do our fighting on the level of consciousness.

The various alphabetic codes and formulas have the power to penetrate the realm of our atoms by penetrating the realm of our consciousness, thereby allowing us to wage war against the Adversary. These Divine Names help us overthrow the Adversary, weakening and gradually eliminating his negative influence on our consciousness. Of course, this is a difficult and challenging task that requires serious meditation, constant effort, and great persistence.

In point of fact, this is precisely what prayer was meant to do. Prayer, from the *Zohar*'s perspective, is a weapon, not a plea to

God. Prayer is a sword, not a supplication. It is a weapon utilized in the one war that truly matters—the war against our Adversary.

The letters of the Aramaic alphabet help us eradicate reactivity. Each time we visually scan a divine Name or recite a particular kabbalistic verse, we weaken the ego. The Names of God banish selfishness. They ignite the consciousness of *certainty* and *conviction*. They provide us with the strength to perform resistance, and thus complete the great task of achieving 100 Percent resistance. Kabbalists are quite emphatic about the fact that we will never conquer the Adversary and achieve *Love Thy Neighbor* without this technology.

The Nanorobots of Manipulation and Transformation

Without question the most powerful sequence of Aramaic letters for battling the reactive consciousness of a human being is the holy *Zohar*. According to the ancient kabbalists, the *Zohar* is the most powerful weapon that mankind possesses for defeating the Adversary and raising human consciousness. The *Zohar* embodies the concealed Light of Immortality that was lost on Mount Sinai after the sin of the Golden Calf.

The Power of the *Zohar*

As I discussed in an earlier chapter, Moses created a second set of Tablets after the first Tablets were shattered. These Second Tablets served as the container for the energy of immortality until such time as mankind earned another opportunity to achieve the ultimate dream. Kabbalists tell us that the *Zohar* itself is that opportunity. In its letters, words, and verses it is the physical manifestation of this energy of immortality.

The *Zohar* is not unlike an electronic encyclopedia stored online, in a non-physical domain. An encyclopedia can come up on your computer screen, or it can be printed out on paper. In paper form it might fill 26 volumes, but it is not the paper that is valuable to us; it is the information that the encyclopedia conveys to our mind by virtue of the letters and words on the page. It's not the liquid ink that is valuable but the knowledge that is transferred to the mind of the reader via the shapes formed by the ink.

If someone wants to learn about chemistry or biology, reading the various inked shapes on the pages transfers knowledge and information about these subjects. This knowledge transcends the physical shape of the inked letters. It's not about the ink. Nor is it about the paper. It's all about the non-physical information that is transferred into your mind through the medium of paper and ink. Ink and paper are merely transfer cables for endless amounts of information and knowledge.

The *Zohar* operates like the encyclopedia in the above example, with one significant difference. Instead of containing information and knowledge, the *Zohar* contains the metaphysical Light and Energy of the *Tree of Life Reality*, including the ultimate energy force known as immortality. The wisdom in the *Zohar* is merely the medium for transfer, just like the encyclopedia's paper and ink. A Divine flow of Energy is transferred to the reader by virtue of the letters, words, verses, and stories printed in the *Zohar*.

The Eyes as Windows to the Soul

The *Zohar* says that when we meditate on or visually scan the letters of its texts, unimaginable energy forces penetrate to the very core our being. Even if you cannot read Aramaic, or do not understand the literal text, the kabbalists of history—Rav Eliezer Papo and Rav Chaim Yosef David Azulai, the grandson of Rav Avraham Azulai, included— tell us a profound effect is achieved by merely making visual contact with the *Zohar*. Naturally, grasping the knowledge of the *Zohar* helps arouse the awesome Forces of Creation. But even if you cannot read a single word, simply meditating on the text generates a flow of energy into your consciousness at a level beyond all your expectations.

Immortality energy raises our consciousness out of the realm where the Adversary's influence holds sway. It devastates the Adversary, destroying reactive traits buried deep within the subconscious mind. From a technological standpoint, there is no other safe or feasible way to affect the atoms in our body. By addressing our being on the level of consciousness, the *Zohar* and the *Names of God* automatically affect every atom, molecule, and cell in the body because consciousness and atoms are one and the same thing.

Thus the Divine Names of God (see Chart on page 214) and the words printed on the pages of the ancient *Zohar* are the Nanorobots of consciousness that will unquestionably lead mankind to its ultimate fate—the removal of chaos and death from human existence.

The *Zohar* in History

Unfortunately, little is known about the *Zohar*'s influence throughout history. Sir Isaac Newton studied the *Zohar* and found in it the source of his great discovery that all the colors of the rainbow are contained in white light. Pope Paul IV authorized the first-ever printing of the *Zohar* in 1558. The Muslims of Morocco, including the late King Hassan II (with whom I studied) drew on the *Zohar* in order to help achieve stability, minimize casualties, and bring about a timely end to the first Gulf War. The honorable Rev. Ezra Stiles, a Congregational clergyman, theologian, and president of Yale College from 1778 to 1795, who corresponded with Thomas Jefferson and Benjamin Franklin, apportioned time each day to study the texts of the *Zohar*, as he himself noted in his diary.

Recognition of the *Zohar*'s metaphysical power came from scientist and scholar alike, mystic and philosopher, Jew, Muslim, and Christian. It is my deepest hope that this book that you are now reading will at last help bring this truth to light for all mankind.

72 NAMES OF GOD

כֹהֵת	אֶכֶא	לֹלֵה	מֹהֹשׁ	עֹלֶם	סִיט	יֹלִי	וֹהוֹ
הֹקֹם	הֹרִי	מֹבֵה	יֹזֵל	הֹהֹע	לֹאוֹ	אֶלֶד	הֹזִי
וֹחֹו	מֹלֹה	יִיִי	נֹלֹך	פֹהֹל	לֹוו	כֶלִי	לֹאוֹ
וֹעִיר	לֹכֶב	אוֹם	רִיי	שֹׁאֹה	יֹרֹת	הֹאֶא	נֹתֹה
יוֹוֹ	רֹהֹע	חֹעֹם	אֹנִי	מֹנֹד	כוֹק	לֹהֹו	יוֹוֹ
מִיֵה	עֹשֹׂל	עֹרִי	סֹאֵל	יֹלֹה	ווֹל	מִיכ	הֹהֹה
פֹוִי	מֹבֵה	נִית	נֹנֹא	עֹמֹם	הוֹשׁ	דֹנִי	וֹהוֹ
מֹוִנִי	עֹנוֹ	יֹהֹה	וֹמֹב	מֹצֹר	הֹרוֹ	יֹיל	נֹמֹם
מוֹם	הֹיִי	יֹבֹם	רֹאֹה	חֹבוֹ	אִיע	מֹנֹק	דֹמֹב

The 72 Names of God are not "names" in any ordinary sense, but a state-of-the-art technology that deeply touches the human soul and is the key to ridding yourself of depression, stress, stagnation, anger, and many other emotional and physical problems. The Names represent a connection to the infinite spiritual current that flows through the Universe. When you correctly bring these power sources together, you are able to gain control over your life and transform it for the better.

PART TEN:

SPEAK TO
THE ATOM

THE DARK SIDE OF CONVENTIONAL NANOROBOTS

Science itself admits that its version of Nanorobots brings great risks to humanity. The reason is clear when viewed through the lens of the *Zohar*. The Nanorobots envisioned by science are merely the *Golden Calf effect*, reappearing in our modern-day world. In other words, these miniscule robots are being programmed to manipulate atoms in order to help bring about immortality the same way the ancient Israelites relied upon the Golden Calf to accomplish the same feat.

Without question, both approaches—the ancient Israelites' and that of contemporary nanotechnologists—absolve the practitioner of all responsibility for transforming human consciousness and, with it, our behavior toward and treatment of our fellow man. A brilliant nanotechnologist, motivated by self-serving interest, is undoubtedly committing the same error as the Israelites on Mount Sinai and, thus, is doomed to fail, according to Kabbalah.

A Golden Nanorobot

The ancient Israelites were not stupid people. On the contrary, they were as advanced in terms of spiritual technology as we are today in the field of computer technology. Just as an individual living a thousand years ago could not possibly fathom computers, cell-phones, movie theaters, HDTV, and biomedical technologies, we cannot possibly fathom the spiritual technologies prevalent during the time of Moses. The Israelites were not naïve enough to believe that worshipping a Golden Calf would yield the same results as God's revelation through the Tablets. The *Zohar* says reading this biblical story in a literal way is absurd. The Golden Calf, from the *Zohar*'s perspective, was not an idol by any means. It was a highly complex instrument, far more sophisticated and powerful than a thousand supercomputers integrated as one. The problem with the Israelites was not their technology. Their problem was their unwillingness to let go of materiality, to let go of the interface (the Calf) that was going to perform the work of generating immortality on their behalf. Because it did not do its work on the level of consciousness, the Golden Calf was not a kabbalistic "Nanorobot."

The Israelites wanted to have their cake and eat it too. Namely, they wanted to achieve immortality for self-seeking reasons without becoming accountable for their behavior and selfish interests. There were no bonds of unconditional love between the Israelites, no consciousness of caring and sharing with their neighbors. It was the Adversary who was in control. This is why the Tablets shattered, why immortality was lost, and why the scourge of death returned to the landscape of humanity.

If today's nanotechnologists are not motivated by the eradication of their ego or the development of unconditional care for their fellow man, if they are motivated by intellectual pursuits, corporate profits, self-interest, self-survival, honor, legacy and a Nobel Prize, then this mode of consciousness will never succeed in achieving immortality in the Universe. We are looking for the same short-cuts that the ancient Israelites pursued.

The Time is Now

The positive aspect of this scenario is that it has become self-evident that we have arrived at that longed-for moment in history when the window to immortality has opened up once again. Just as Moses' approach to immortality—which was to lose one's ego—competed against the Israelites' approach, which was to retain ego and utilize a material intermediary, the same scenario is playing out today. The same skepticism the Israelites had for Moses affects scientists—*and all of us*—when it comes to believing that our consciousness and behavior are actually a cutting-edge technology. Mankind didn't get it then, and we are in danger of not getting it now.

Kabbalah is advocating Moses' approach to immortality—which involves embracing the technology known as *Love Thy Neighbor*—because this behavior is mirrored in the subatomic and atomic world with every atom in our body. Both the Israelites and Moses understood that immortality was attainable. They merely utilized competing technologies, one of which had no hope of success, whereas the other had its success written into the blueprint of Creation.

Then is Now

Today the same set of circumstances plays out before our very eyes. Scientists have embraced a subject that was once considered taboo; they have developed a technology for achieving the end of death. Likewise, Kabbalah has once again arrived on the world scene after thousands of years of concealment, also promising us a technology that can bring about the death of death.

One would think that news of these two competing technologies—conventional nanotechnology versus kabbalistic nanotechnology—and the goal they both seek would have set the world on fire. The news should be rippling throughout the global media, generating uncontainable excitement and hope. But it isn't, thanks to the effectiveness of the Adversary. And unfortunately, thus far nanotechnologists are going the route of the Golden Calf, working on creating robots to manipulate atoms instead of transforming their own consciousness.

NANOROBOTS OUT OF CONTROL

Science posits that a single Nanorobot must be equipped with the ability to self-replicate. This is necessary due to the inconceivable number of atoms in every square inch of our body. You would need trillions of Nanorobots just to manipulate all the molecules and atoms in one small area. Science does not have enough time or resources to build a trillion Nanorobots, so it has hit on the clever but dangerous solution of self-replication.

By creating one self-replicating Nanorobot, one could suddenly turn into two, and then four, then eight, sixteen, thirty-two, sixty-four, etc. In just a matter of minutes, this exponential doubling creates billions of Nanorobots, and therein lies the risk and the danger. Imagine something goes wrong with the computer program inside these Nanorobots, if the software crashes or malfunctions, these Nanorobots could theoretically keep on self-replicating to the point of overwhelming the Earth and covering it in what scientists call *ecophagy*, or "grey goo." It's a frightening end-of-the-world scenario that may be all too likely.

Science journalist Philip Ball explained the word *ecophagy* is an article from issue 2386 of *New Scientist* magazine, 15th of March 2003, pg 50:

> *"They call it 'global ecophagy.' That's 'eating the Earth' to you and me. Rumor has it that this is what replicating nanostructures might do, and according to one estimate, they could gobble up the entire planet in about three hours flat."*

Imagine Nanorobots replicating so fast that after just 180 minutes they literally swallow up the entire Earth! Both scientists and politicians are now raising the obvious next question: *What if nanotechnology fell into the hands of terrorists?*

Clearly, there is a dark side to science's version of nanotechnology. This dark side exists because science is only addressing Phase Two; it seeks the ultimate goal of immortality by employing the wrong technology. Phase Two addresses only the physical world, which the Adversary controls. In the realm of the Adversary, the realm of the *Tree of Knowledge Good and Evil*, every positive side also has a dark side, which is why nanotechnology holds such great promise and great danger. But in the realm of the nonphysical *Tree of Life Reality*, the realm of consciousness, there is only the positive side. If you control the consciousness level—

Phase One—you control the entire physical world and, in turn, you control the Adversary. Therein lies the power of the *Zohar*, and of Kabbalah's version of nanotechnology.

SPEAK!

> "And speak to the rock before their eyes; and it shall give forth its water . . . Moses raised his hand and struck the rock with his staff twice, when an abundance of water gushed forth, and the congregation and their livestock drank."
> —Numbers 20:8, 11

For those not familiar with this section of the Bible, it concerns an event that took place after the Revelation on Mount Sinai. Immortality was now lost, and the Israelites were wandering the desert crying out for water. God instructs Moses to speak to a rock in front of all the Israelites, allowing water to flow out of it. Surprisingly, Moses does not listen. Instead of speaking to the rock, Moses takes his rod and strikes the rock twice. Then water begins to flow.

We're told that God then punished Moses for disobeying His command. Moses' punishment was that he could not enter into the Land of Israel. And so it was that Moses eventually died and came to be buried in an unknown grave outside the Holy Land.

The *Zohar* decodes this story, telling us that water never flowed out of the rock. The Bible, on a deeper level, was never even referring to drinking water. Water is a metaphor for the wisdom, divine energy, and technology of Kabbalah. The *Zohar* states:

> *At the second striking of the rock these drops of water came out. These drops of water are hints of wisdom, hints of the wisdom of Kabbalah.*
> —*Zohar* Vol. 22, 16:73

It was not water dripping out of the rock, but rather the awesome energy and power of Kabbalah. The *Zohar* goes on to explain that drops of water issued from the rock instead of a wave. Why?

A Second Chance at Paradise

The master kabbalists of history tell us that Moses did not really disobey God. And God did not really punish Moses by preventing him from entering the Holy Land. Moses represents *Zeir Anpin* or the *Tree of Life Reality*. The phrase *Land of Israel* is code for the physical realm, or the dimension of *Malkhut*. The inner meaning of this unusual story concerns our physical world and its inability to bond with the *Tree of Life Reality* to achieve immortality (signified by Moses not being able to enter the Holy Land). The question that must be raised is why? Why was Moses unable to enter the Holy Land? Why was our physical Earth still unable to connect to the Light Force of the Creator?

The answer to this question is found in the actions of Moses. God told Moses to *speak* to the rock. But Moses chose to strike the rock instead. This action is a reflection of the consciousness of the Israelites—not that of Moses. Speaking to the rock is not a physical action. Speaking is the byproduct of consciousness, of thought expressing itself in words. God was telling Moses to use the power of consciousness to bond this Universe with the Light Force of the *Tree of Life*. But the Israelites were still refusing to let go of ego consciousness, so Moses used a physical action—striking the rock with his rod—in order to draw down the Light of Immortality (drops of water dripping from the rock).

SPEAK, NOT STRIKE!

Kabbalah calls upon us to speak to the atom, not to strike the atom. Conventional Nanorobots are designed to strike the atom directly, to manipulate it in order to rebuild body tissues, cells, and organs. But this kind of physical consciousness will never achieve the ultimate objective. We must *speak* to the atom through the power of our consciousness.

We speak to the atom by virtue of the transformation of our consciousness from self-centered receiving into simple sharing. Using the *Zohar* and the *Names of God*, we ignite nothing less than the awesome Light Force of the Creator in our consciousness, body, and soul. Now our consciousness speaks directly to each and every atom, because our consciousness and our atoms are one and the same. Each time we open a page of the *Zohar*, or meditate upon a *Name of God*, we use consciousness to literally penetrate every atom (particle of consciousness) that permeates our being and thereby weaken the power of the Adversary.

Eye to Eye

For those of us who cannot read or speak the language of the *Zohar*, visual meditation is akin to speaking to the atoms. We know this to be a great and powerful secret, for we find it confirmed in both the *Zohar* and the Bible in regard to the Revelation that took place on Mount Sinai. The Bible tells us that the Israelites who witnessed this great event actually *saw the sounds* associated with God's Revelation:

> *"And all the people could see the sounds."*
> —Exodus 20:15

The *Zohar* unravels this radical concept further. As the Divine energy flowed out of the Tablets after traveling through all ten dimensions, the *Zohar* says the words uttered by God made thunderous sounds that could actually be *seen* by the Israelites.

> *That sound was divided into seventy sounds and they all illuminated and sparkled before the eyes of all the Israelites, who saw His splendor eye-to-eye.*
> —*Zohar* Vol. 11, 33:368

Herein lies one of the great secrets behind the idea of scanning biblical and kabbalistic texts, specifically the *Zohar*, known as the *Book of Splendor*: our eyes have the power to see sounds, to perceive the energy waves and vibrations created by the very letters and words used to form a sound. To see the Divine Names and the sacred texts of the *Zohar* is to also speak their sounds.

Thus each of us must speak to our atoms, not strike them, when trying to restore our bodies and souls to their original state of well being. Each time we behave with egocentric consciousness we are striking our atoms, weakening their bonds, and making them more susceptible to the negative influences of our environment: the toxic air we breathe; the unhealthy foods we eat; and the tainted waters that we drink. Every time we treat a symptom we strike the atom. Thus we are only unleashing drops of energy instead of a constant flow of Light.

Speak to the atom—do not strike it! Through the technology of *Love Thy Neighbor* and by utilizing instruments like the *Zohar*, we can reclaim control of our thoughts and, in turn, our bodies and souls.

Practically Speaking

Resisting a simple act of selfishness each day of our lives is to speak to our atoms on the simplest of levels. Resist an urge to scream at a loved one. Resist the natural reflex to curse those who offend you or hurt you. Resist losing your temper, even when it seems justified. Most importantly, speaking to our atoms means recognizing the existence and influence of the Adversary. This recognition is extremely tough on the ego. That is a clue that you have identified the true culprit. This is how we raise consciousness. This is consciousness. And it rises as you force yourself to think of others, to consider them even though every impulse in your body tells you otherwise.

If we can spot ego in our actions, question our motives, see our hidden agendas, and at least strive to change our behavior in small ways each day, we are taking giant leaps in the quantum realm. Instead of focusing on being smart or right in an argument or debate, we focus on identifying our self-centered response in the situation. After all, the purpose of life is not to win an argument and be right. It's to reveal Light through resistance.

The Fruit Contains the Seed

Make no mistake about it, the ultimate goal of eternal happiness will be achieved regardless of our behavior. The moment the Creator decided to impart unending happiness to the Vessel, it was a *fait accompli*. The end result was present in the Original Thought. Only time creates the illusion that we have not yet arrived at that predestined moment. Time exists to give us free will, which allows us to earn the merit that only accrues when we accomplish a task by virtue of our own effort.

We either reach our destination through unspeakable suffering, as we have been doing for thousands of years, or we take the fight inward, waging war on our own selfish indulgent impulses through authentic nanotechnology—a path filled with countless blessings. Ultimately both lead to the same destination

One Choice

Simply stated, exercising our free will means choosing one of two paths to the final destination: the path of pain for the ego and love for our fellow man, or the path of gratifying the ego, accompanied by long-term chaos and suffering.

The choice is ours to make.

THE OPPORTUNITY FOR BIOLOGICAL IMMORTALITY

Admittedly, I feel tremendous excitement over the stunning developments taking place in the field of conventional nanotechnology, for they are a sign that we are on the verge of achieving the ultimate goal. Science is now openly and seriously discussing the topic of immortality, seeing it as possible during the next twenty to fifty years. Clearly, science is tuning in to the imperceptible metaphysical forces swirling in the cosmos, confirming what my master knew to be true forty years ago—that the forces of immortality and the revelation of the full measure of the Light Force is at hand.

In order to manifest this opportunity we have been given the gift of Kabbalah, an ancient science and technology that can help us regain what Moses attained, the technology for bonding ourselves with the *Tree of Life Reality*, but this time permanently.

Both the Bible and the *Zohar* tell us that in the End of Days, when our Final Redemption is ready to become manifest, all people, young and old, will understand the secret of *Love Thy Neighbor* and the mysteries of life. The knowledge and insights presented throughout this book provide us with that opportunity. For the first time in human history, the layperson can now discover where we came from, where the atom came from, why death occurs, and how immortality can be achieved through the chemical bonds between atoms. You are living proof, for you have just discovered it.

Unquestionably, we have arrived at the moment of our Final Redemption. Immortality is here right now. And the power is absolutely in your hands. If you don't feel it in the depth of your soul, perhaps you should read this book one more time. If you do feel it, if you sense the power and secrets behind what you've just read, well then, all I can say is this: Your neighbor awaits.

The Fulfillment of a Promise

Earlier in this book, I promised to share the kabbalistic solution to the paradox that vexed the scientists Loschmidt and Boltzmann. This is the core of our concluding chapter, which is, perhaps, the most important of this entire book.

PART ELEVEN:

THE
BOMBSHELL!
(A Paradox Resolved)

THE SOLUTION IN
THE SEED

I am purposely trying to emulate the spirit of science in this following attempt to reduce the wisdom of Kabbalah to its simplest elements. If I am successful, it should ignite nothing less than a people's movement whose sole objective is to bring about the unequivocal downfall of death, the end of all unhappiness, and the advent of immortality. For if you make a sincere attempt to grasp the simple kabbalistic truths summarized here—logical proofs that reconcile science with Kabbalah—the Cause and purpose of all reality will become self-evident.

Origins

There has been a fierce ongoing debate throughout human history over the very nature of reality. Today, many physicists claim that exotic subatomic particles or vibrating strings lie at the heart of the Universe. Others, like mathematician and astronomer Sir James Jeans have a different view:

> "The Universe begins to look more like a great thought than a great machine."

We will now employ kabbalistic reasoning to discover the ultimate cause of reality, and thereby answer the single most important question ever—a question that has haunted mankind since time immemorial.

The Thought of Creation

Kabbalah has often been described as the most comprehensive science of Cause and Effect known to man. By employing this ancient kabbalistic rule of Cause and Effect, we will crack the mysteries surrounding the nature of reality and the cause of all existence in one fell swoop.

Tragically, when one considers the amount of bloodshed, conflict, and pain that this topic has caused, the simplicity of the logic behind the answer is quite staggering. It's been right in front of our noses the entire time.

A primary rule of the science of Cause and Effect states the following:

> **The Cause always contains the Effect,**
> **and the Effect always contains the Cause.**

Let us take a closer look at the first aspect of this rule.

An apple seed—*the Cause*—always contains the entire tree—*the Effect*—within it. You cannot see the Final Effect when observing the Original Seed but nonetheless the complete tree is present within it.

Let us now examine the second aspect to this rule: *The Effect always contains the Cause.* The final state of an apple tree is, inevitably, the apple that dangles from a branch. Within the apple we find the Final Effect—another apple seed. Hence, the Final Effect (the apple seed) contains the Original Cause (the original apple seed).

Disappearance of the Original Seed

The original Cause of the tree—*the seed*—disappears when the tree materializes. The individual no longer perceives the Original Seed (and Cause) with the five senses. However, one is able to find the Cause *within the Final Effect*: Lo and behold, another apple seed is contained within the apple!

Ergo, by studying the Final Effect, one is able to move *backward* in *time* to find the Original *Cause* of the Effect.

To summarize: A seed is buried in the ground. An apple tree emerges. The Original Seed is now invisible, but we find it again in the Final Effect—the seed inside the apple. Thus the Cause may be extrapolated simply by investigating the Effect.

Mankind can therefore find the Original Cause of all existence by observing the Final Effect.

The Cause of All Existence

Man correlates to the apple. Within man we find self-awareness and consciousness, the highest and Final Effect of existence. Why? It is consciousness that allows us to recognize and ponder our own existence. And if consciousness is the final effect, an Original Force of consciousness is thereby the Cause of all existence.

We have deduced our answer. Consciousness created the Universe and everything in it.

The Seed of an Apple, the Seed of Man

The apple seed analogy may be extended further. We can ask: What is the *consciousness* of an apple seed, or what is the apple's genetic purpose? The answer is obvious: *creating an apple tree.*

If an apple seed is the Final Effect in an apple, then in human beings a man's sperm and a woman's ovum (egg) are the Final Effect. What then is the consciousness of the male sperm and female egg? Once again the answer is clear: to unite as one in an act of creation embodied by infinite pleasure and ecstacy. Thus, the original Cause and consciousness behind all existence is the act of Creation itself, which is the sharing and experience of inexpressible joy.

And so we have come full circle, back to the beginning of the Creation story recounted earlier in the book, confirming the original Thought of Creation: God emanated Light for one great purpose—to create and then fill the Vessel with infinite pleasure. This is, according to the *Zohar*, the purpose of Creation.

We now understand that consciousness is the Cause of all existence, and its purpose is to share endless pleasure with the souls of humanity.

THE SEED OF IMMORTALITY

After this light was created, it was concealed and enclosed within that covenant that entered the rose and fructified it. This is referred to as "a tree bearing fruit whose seed is within it."
—*Zohar*, Vol. 1, Prologue, The Rose

When we study the Effect, one more compelling and definitive insight emerges concerning the ultimate purpose of Creation. Sperm and ova (eggs) are undeniably immortal, according to biology. Biologists now understand that they are made up of germinal cells that never die, as opposed to the rest of our body, which is composed of somatic cells. All somatic cells wind up aging and inevitably committing virtual suicide, which is why the body dies, according to medical science.

This tells us that immortality is also found in the Ultimate Effect, thereby leading us to the conclusion that immortality must also be the ultimate purpose of all existence. This is the secret of the above quote from the *Zohar*, which says Light was concealed and enclosed within the Covenant (reproductive organs) where it entered the rose (female reproductive organ) and fructified it. Immortality has been temporarily relegated to this particular region of the human anatomy and it expresses itself in the immortal chain of human existence and our genes. No one man (as of yet) lives forever, but the chain itself continues through the concept known as *a tree bearing fruit whose seed is within it*. This is the secret that was handed down from kabbalists to their closest and worthiest students over the generations.

Kabbalists, through the wisdom of Kabbalah, possess the formula for unlocking the forces of immortality that reside within the sperm and ovum so that the body and the entire world can achieve immortality.

Why Death?

Kabbalah and science tell us that our current physical body—on a cellular level— is designed to be temporary. Biology tells us the body only stays alive long enough to ensure the transmission and continuation of our immortal genes, which are passed on through the cells that create sperm and ova. Once this has been achieved there is no further use for the body, so it gradually ages and dies.

However, from the kabbalistic viewpoint, there is a priceless secret hidden within this process. The secret is that death itself must *also* be a temporary phenomenon, because the Effect contains the Cause, so if the body is temporary, death itself must be temporary. Kabbalistically, the body in its current state is merely a transitory means of bringing about the Final Effect: eternal pleasure achieved through the union of two opposites—in this case, male and female—into one eternal state of happiness.

The obvious question is, *When*? When will death finally end, and immortality begin? How do we stop the temporary cycle of bodily death? Why does the cycle keep repeating? Why do we keep dying, while our genes and germinal cells remain immortal? How do we unleash the immortality contained within the sperm and ovum so that it permeates the entire body and all existence?

Kabbalistically, the body is the electron. It embodies the consciousness of a selfish, relentless negative-charged *Desire to Receive*. This is why the electron creates the illusion of physical matter by virtue of its motion and negative charge. Just as the rotor of a fan spins fast enough to produce the illusion that there is no gap between the blades, the motion of the electron creates the illusion of solid matter.

We are here to gradually transform the body by sharing with others and *this is why* the body exists. The *Desire to Receive* is what causes death, for it disconnects us from the Source of Life by virtue of its opposition to the state of the Light. Physical existence and the multitudes of people on this planet give us the opportunity to effect a transformation by *resisting* selfishness and learning to share unconditionally with the other members (bodies) of society. Until that transformation is complete, death will remain part of human existence, and immortality will remain hidden inside the germinal chain of human existence.

The Selfish Gene to the Selfless Gene

Richard Dawkins, the brilliant biologist and science writer, acknowledges that *selfishness* is behind the propagation of our genes. He says the body is merely a means to achieve this end, and it serves no other purpose. Kabbalists concur wholeheartedly, and the *Zohar* declared this scientific truth 2000 years ago. Dawkins, ironically, also confirmed the kabbalistic solution to the end of death, although Dawkins himself did not perceive the magnificent profundity of his ideas.

The Power of the Science of Kabbalah

Specifically, three key concepts can be extrapolated from Kabbalah that have the power to unleash a transformation in physics and biology beyond all current imagining.

THREE CONCEPTS

There is nothing that appears within human civilization that does not first begin in the realm of consciousness. Consciousness always precedes physical expression, without fail. Everything from art to literature, from science to technology, all the physical manifestations emerging from the preceding fields of human activity *first* began as an idea. An idea or a thought is defined as part of the *realm of consciousness*. The same principle holds true with atoms, electrons, and protons. They are merely manifestations of consciousness. Consciousness is the singular thread that weaves through all Creation. This is the first concept.

The final two concepts for understanding the natural world relate directly to the nature of consciousness. Specifically, there is one *law* that governs the realm of consciousness and there is one *force* that influences consciousness. We have examined both throughout the course of this book. The moment we truly understand the one law and the one force, all paradoxes in physics are reconciled; all conflicts vanish.

The One Law

The one law states that in the realm of consciousness *like attracts like, and opposites repel.* This is all we need to know. Everything that occurs in our reality flows from this one law.

The One Force

The one force that influences consciousness is an opposing power, a countervailing force that uses the one law to conceal itself, and thus propels this world toward increasing chaos. The one force is called Satan. As we've discovered, the word Satan is the most corrupted and misunderstood word in the human language. Translated properly it means *Adversary.* *Adversary* refers to a force that relentlessly propels this world—and our individual selves—away from the Source of true reality. Since true reality is perfect order, the further we move away from it, and the greater the distance and space, the greater the increase in disorder.

Thus the Adversary is the Cause of the increasing disorder that occurs in this physical domain. On the individual level, the Adversary impels us to *receive* instead of share, and it is this act of receiving that distances us from the Source of perfect order and happiness. Let's now address the Loschmidt Paradox and discover how a subatomic realm where time and molecules move forward *and backwards* gives birth to a reality where time and molecules move in but one direction, toward what appears to be increasing chaos, as stated in the second law of thermodynamics.

TRUE REALITY

True reality is a realm of Light. The Light is pure, boundless consciousness and it encompasses an incalculable, inexhaustible happiness. The Light created a Vessel—the souls of humankind—to impart this happiness forever through the union of two opposites: Sharing and Receiving, Light and Vessel. In the realm of consciousness however, it is impossible to unite opposites because of the law that states *opposites repel*. Hence, the first paradox appears: How does God share happiness with humanity if humanity's *Desire to Receive* is the actual culprit behind the separation of these two forms of consciousness?

The answer was revealed in the story of the wealthy miser Sal Fishman and the homeless drifter. The drifter's physical act of receiving was actually an act of sharing. He *received* on the level of physicality, but he *shared* on the level of consciousness. This story reveals the key to uniting the Light and Vessel: the Vessel must receive physically, *but for the sake of sharing on the level of consciousness*.

THE ANSWER WITHIN

We learned that the DNA of God was implanted within the Vessel. This DNA is actually a kind of cosmic wormhole, a Light-filled passageway into the Endless World. The Vessel cannot connect to the Divine Light within itself because of the Law of Attraction, which states that *opposites repel*. So the Vessel has no way to get back *home*—figuratively and literally speaking—and reunite with God. This is like the atom, where the electron cannot connect to the proton of the same atom.

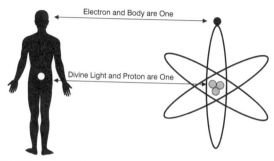

Body cannot connect to Divine Light just as the Electron cannot connect to Proton because *Opposites Repel*. The only way to reduce the space is to emulate the Light. Thus we need other people (and our atoms require other atoms) to bridge the gulf from darkness to Light, death to immortality. When *like attracts like* in the level of consciousness, *opposites attract* in the physical world.

As an aside, we can now begin to understand the origins of those well-known phrases: *Happiness is within. God is within. Everyone is a spark of the Divine.* While these sentiments are true on the face of it, the full magnitude of these ideas has not yet been grasped by humanity.

LOCATING THE AUTHENTIC CREATOR

According to Kabbalah, if you keep dividing subatomic particles until you finally reach the Ultimate Source, you will reach a brilliant infinite realm of pure luminous energy, an endless dimension of stunning, radiant divine consciousness, infinitely more authentic than our physical reality.

Looking within to find happiness is not just an abstract pearl of wisdom. It is technology, plain and simple. The God that everyone seeks, the ultimate truth that we all search for, is literally within the inner space of reality. Kabbalah says there are ten inner dimensions that must be traversed to reach the Endless Realm that lies within. It can hardly be coincidence that the superstring theory of physics requires ten dimensions to reconcile our macroscopic world with the subatomic quantum world. Both Kabbalah and physics are describing the same reality, but science stops short. Science has found the electron, but it has not yet found the essence of the electron—*consciousness*—even though it is staring science right in the face.

How, then, can a physicist and a layperson find the ultimate truth? How can we, fragments of the Vessel, return home? How does the Vessel find happiness and immortality if it cannot possibly reach the God within because of its opposite nature?

The Only Solution

The connection to the Light Force of the Creator is made one single way: the individual must emulate God's consciousness and God's actions, which means to share and love one another unconditionally. This is how one moves closer to, connects with, and experiences the God within. This is the law that states *like attracts like*. When we do this in the realm of consciousness, we can direct how opposites attract in our physical reality. If we have chaos, we attract the opposite—perfect order. If we have sickness, we attract healing. If we have poverty, we attract sustenance. If we are jealous, we attract inner security. If we have a question, we attract the true answer.

There is no other methodology for receiving the blessings and Light of the Creator. No matter how well-intentioned we are, or how hard we pray, we cannot connect to the God within as long as our body and consciousness are in an opposite state of receiving. This is why the Vessel was forced to shatter into pieces. Only by interacting with others, specifically through the act of sharing and learning how to love unconditionally, can we ever make contact with the Creator within and achieve the purpose of Creation—immortality and eternal pleasure.

This is the reason for the existence of the body. It exists *temporarily* to give us an opportunity to transform its consciousness from *receiving* (selfish gene) into *Receiving for the Sake of Sharing* (the selfless God Gene). Immortality was put into a holding pattern within the sperm and ovum until this transformation is complete.

The World Matters

The *Zohar* says everything in our Universe—from inanimate objects to the vegetable and animal kingdoms—is all under the direct influence of the Light of the Creator and the Divine consciousness. Thus, every atom bonds through the familiar physical law where *opposites attract* and *like forces repel*. But this is only the physical Effect. The *consciousness* of the atom is to share an electron in order to fulfill another atom that is short an electron. And the consciousness of the receiving atom is to accept electrons from an atom in order to help the donating atom achieve its own stability and *happiness*.

This interaction on the physical level causes the first atom to be positive and the second atom to be negative as a result of having more electrons than the first atom. But under this same scenario, both atoms display a sharing consciousness and therefore *like and attracts like*. In turn, both atoms bond through the physical effect of opposites attracting.

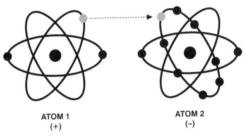

ATOM 1
(+)

ATOM 2
(−)

CONSCIOUSNESS: Atom 1 *shares* and electron. Atom 2 receives for the *Sake of Sharing* causing like to attract like

PHYSICALLY: Atom 1 shares an electron with atom 2 causing opposites to attract

As we can now understand, there are two forces at work—*like attracts like* and *opposites attract!* The former gives birth to the latter. Science is absolutely correct when it says opposites attract. Kabbalah is also correct when it states opposites repel. The two worlds are reconciled once you factor in consciousness.

Continental Divide

There is a vast gulf between the God within and our physical bodies. This is why it is so difficult for us to find Divinity and experience constant blessings. The only way to make contact and find truth is to first remove the gulf, to renounce self-interest and embrace selflessness. But we find this impossible to do. We are overwhelmed with skepticism and doubt because we do not recognize the Adversary. However, once we cross that line, the moment we reduce our ego and alter our belief system—even temporarily—to just consider the possibility that this opposing force indeed exists, we then begin to perceive the flickering lights of truth, far off in the distance.

THE SECRET

The only way to make contact with the God Gene within is to share with each other. Each external act of sharing moves us closer to God because *like attracts like*. When sharing is viewed in this manner, we will grasp what *Enlightened Greed* is really all about, and it will become the motivation behind our acts of sharing and our acts of resistance.

The State of the World is a State of Mind

Whether our entire world—environmentally and socially—moves closer to the Light or drifts further into darkness is determined solely by the sum total of our interactions with one another. The collective state of human consciousness determines the state of the world. There is no more profound insight in all of human history than this.

Why Resistance is Sharing

When photons from the sun travel 91 million miles to reach this planet, space itself remains black, even though sunlight is streaming through space en route to our planet. This strange effect of black sunlight is due to the lack of resistance in space. Space is a vacuum, therefore there is nothing to resist and reflect the photons. But when invisible photons radiating from the sun strike our planet, the Earth resists the photons. Magically, light appears. The same principle holds true with Divine Light. When we resist it, we are reflecting it outward, and thus Light goes on in our life and we perceive the hidden truths within.

When, however, we are governed by ego and self-interest, there is no resistance and, thus, we fail to find the truth concerning consciousness as the Source of all reality. We fail to find happiness for we are floundering in spiritual darkness. The solution is to resist ego.

It's All About the Adversary

If we can admit that our behavior is motivated by self-interest, if we can admit that there is a force called the Adversary, we are now being proactive instead of reactive, sharing instead of receiving. To prevent that from occurring, the Adversary uses unrelenting force. You will know if you have achieved resistance if you are able to see the hand of the Adversary at work. This is the litmus test. If you resist, you will unquestionably receive Light in your life, and you will begin to perceive truths you never perceived before. The proof must be in the pudding. In Kabbalah, there is no blind faith. Genuine results are the only yardstick.

REALITY, CREDIT CARDS, AND LIFE

Imagine a person named Bob who has zero money in his bank account. The name of the game is simple: Bob must accumulate as much cash in his account as possible. The easiest thing for our friend Bob to do is to borrow $10,000 from a credit card company. In the short term Bob is succeeding in accumulating cash. However, Bob is also in debt, and there is a hefty interest rate on the money that he is borrowing. If Bob keeps this up, the very money he is accumulating will serve to bankrupt him, and leave him not just penniless but homeless too.

Bob has an alternative. Instead of first receiving money, Bob can decide to first invest time and devote energy into building something. There is no immediate reward since effort is first required. But after a while money starts coming in, and Bob can then deposit that money into the bank.

Life is that Simple

Though these two scenarios are simplistic, the truth they underscore is frighteningly real. In this example money is the Light of the Creator. The moment we start taking instead of sharing, we accumulate immediate happiness, but we are increasing our debt at the same time. This debt is space. Negative space. If we keep taking without sharing, the very pleasure we derive from our receiving winds up killing us.

We think we're smart. We are not. There is no Angel of Death. There is only space. Space is created when we take instead of share, when we indulge our ego instead of resisting it. We eventually create so much space within ourselves that we lose complete contact with the God Force within (often called the human soul) and our molecules fall apart.

Pain is Payment

Any pain in our life, any chaos in our life, is a direct result of the space we've created from years of taking. We borrowed from the Universe and left a black hole. That hole grows larger each time we indulge our ego and receive instead of sharing. Business, industry, education, government are all founded upon receiving instead of sharing, which is why society decays, and yet we remain blind to the underlying cause behind the degradation of human life, civilization, and the global environment. These are just manifestations of the negative space that we have created by simple human behavior. This has been the path of history.

The Art of Deception

Lacking the teachings of Kabbalah, this negative space dupes us when we do perform a sharing action. We are left wondering why there seemed to be no true benefit. The situation becomes dangerous when we make the all too common mistake of complaining over the lack of reward for sharing, for now we have fallen under the influence of the Adversary.

Even if our original act was pure, our complaining is a form of receiving, which allows space to return. Our world winds up looking hopeless, so we become even more desperate to fill the emptiness, and the vicious cycle perpetuates. The Adversary is the one who convinces us that sharing doesn't pay, and that losing the ego is too terrifying a thought to consider. In addition, he gives us temporary relief so we're not motivated to pay off our debt. On the contrary, we increase it.

Paying Down the Loan

If we embrace the opportunity and recognize it for what it is, the space fills in quickly, and we can change our lives by changing our consciousness. Once those spaces are filled, our sharing actions bring us blessings beyond measure, at the same speed that we acquired our debt.

LIGHT IS MERCY

Students often ask if there is a way to reduce the pain that we are owed as a result of the space that we ourselves created. The answer is an emphatic *yes*.

Moses was given the technology of Kabbalah on Mount Sinai, which can empower us with the strength, the wisdom, and the will to share and resist the ego.

The Sinai Plan

The technology revealed at Sinai was designed to allow us to pay our debts back in a way where we could still enjoy life, thanks to friendships, partnerships, marriages, and children—in a word, *relationships*. If we appreciated this, and used the Light to uproot our ego, only the ego would suffer—not the body and soul, and certainly not the world around us. Moreover, the Light we would generate would break up our payments into smaller increments so that they would become easier to manage. I will now explain how this works.

Judgment Tempered with Mercy

Suppose someone pointed the finger of blame towards other people all of his life. In addition, he continually pointed his finger by gossiping and slandering people behind their backs. This individual has now created a specific measure of space with his finger. Suppose it's now time for payment. Let's say the payment for the finger is equal to five minutes in a burning candle flame. The heat of the fire would create space between the molecules, causing the finger to burn.

However, if this person decided to use the path of Kabbalah to pay back the debt, it would work as follows. Instead of time working against the individual in a judgmental fashion, keeping the finger in the flame for five straight minutes, time can be made to work in the individual's favor. The interjection of Light allows the finger to stay in the candle flame for only two-second intervals, alternating with thirty-second pauses of Light. Now time is helping the individual as opposed to hurting him, just as the forest was consumed by fire in our earlier chapter.

This pattern continues until the two-second intervals eventually total five minutes. The Universal Law of Cause and Effect, and the cosmic justice system have now been satisfied. And during those thirty-second intervals, the individual was able to enjoy his family, his friends, and the world. The person's path to the redemption of his finger has been filled with blessings and appreciation, motivated by a sincere desire to change his consciousness forever. This is how Light and sharing actions cause time to be used in a merciful manner.

This method of repayment is available to everyone if their heart is true and their intent to pay back is authentic.

THE BIGGEST SECRET OF ALL

No words can express my appreciation for the secret I share within these pages. This is the secret handed down through the kabbalists since the time of Mount Sinai. I pray that the entire world, will immediately understand the power of what I am about to reveal. This secret was guarded tightly until the arrival of Kabbalist Rav Yehuda Ashlag. His beloved and sainted disciple, Rav Yehuda Brandwein, my master, created an environment in which we could ready ourselves for the revelation of this secret.

And I was given the task, with my partner in body and soul, Karen, to share it with the world.

The Zohar is the Light of immortality that was lost on Mount Sinai. How can a book contain metaphysical energy or non-tangible Light? How can a book contain immortality? Because immortality is a state of consciousness. Once you possess the right consciousness, you have it. The *Zohar* reveals the actions that leads a person to achieve immortality. When those actions are taken, motivated by the right consciousness, immortality happens by itself. With sweetness. With kindness. With gentleness. With hope. With joy. With fulfillment beyond words. Without any physical death or fear. That is how it works.

This Light was infused into the *Zohar* until such time that mankind paid back the debt and removed all space. The ancient kabbalists tell us that the *Zohar*'s emergence into the general public is a sign that the Light of the Creator (the Light within each of us) is ready to shine eternally.

There was such a window that appeared during the Middle Ages. Unfortunately, people were not yet ready to sacrifice their egos. Organized religion, particularly the rabbinical establishment, went to great lengths to conceal the *Zohar* and suppress the truth of what was discovered. Religious authorities accused the kabbalists of being charlatans, thieves, and liars. Some even began a smear campaign, calling the *Zohar* a fake and forgery. All of this played out against a backdrop of brutality, during which time Muslims, Christians, and Jews were massacred. Space—materializing as the death of millions—ruled the landscape.

Another window of opportunity stands before us now and it is wide open. Today the *Zohar* is reaching millions of people for the first time in human history. The *Zohar*, by its mere presence, is injecting metaphysical Light into our existence.

One Lesson to Be Learned

If you take home but one idea from this book, only one lesson, if it opened your heart and your mind to the great gift before us, then let the understanding of the power of the *Zohar* eradicate the pain and space in your life. **The more the Light of the *Zohar* illuminates our world, the more we banish the darkness and the more pleasant our path to transformation becomes.** This is the secret. Darkness and Light cannot coexist. If you light a candle in a dark room, the darkness disappears. The Light of the *Zohar* lights up the darkness of this world. Sharing the *Zohar* with another human being is, without question, the greatest act of sharing a man or woman can achieve in this physical reality. If we emulate the Light, we achieve oneness with the Light then the fears and the wars and the machinations in our minds simply will not materialize.

The Wonderland Effect

By virtue of receiving, we created distance between our self and the Light-filled, timeless, motionless reality of perfect order. This distance was so great that we wound up in an opposite reality. We stepped into Alice in Wonderland's proverbial looking-glass as a result of receiving consciousness and wound up in a vast, dark Universe where the laws of physics are the opposite of true reality.

Our distance begat the forces of time, space, motion, and increasing disorder, all features directly and indirectly related to the second law of thermodynamics.

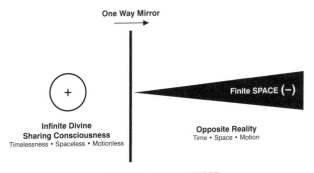

One Way Mirror

+

Finite SPACE (−)

**Infinite Divine
Sharing Consciousness**
Timelessness • Spaceless • Motionless

Opposite Reality
Time • Space • Motion

THE WONDERLAND EFFECT

Our Universe is a mirror of true reality. Instead of Light, there is darkness. Instead of timelessness, there is time. Instead of order, there is chaos. On one side of the mirror, the original single energy force of receiving or negative consciousness is pure energy. On the other side of the mirror we find the opposite as it congeals into countless particles of matter the science dubs the electron.

Two Sides of the Mirror

Let's examine the two mirror Universes:

- On one side of the mirror there is energy. On the other side is the opposite state, which is matter.
- On one side of the mirror this energy is made up of pure consciousness. On the other side it appears as meaningless matter.
- On one side of the mirror we find Light. On the other there is darkness.
- On one side of the mirror there is no space or time. On the other side we find the space-time continuum.
- On one side of the mirror, reality is fused with purpose.

On the other side, matter, the forces of nature and human existence appear aimless.

- On one side of the mirror we find perfect order. On the other side we find utter chaos.
- On one side of the mirror we find oneness. On the other side we find a multitude of forces and subatomic particles.
- On one side of the mirror we find infinite happiness and pleasure. On the other side we find sadness and pain.
- On one side of the mirror we find infinite luminous inner space. On the other side we find the illusion of infinite, pitch-black outer space.
- On one side of the mirror we find the true Divine Light of God. On the other side we find superstition and myth.
- On one side of the mirror we find immortality. On the other side we find death.

The degree of chaos and darkness that we experience is determined by our state of consciousness, which establishes our position relative to the hidden reality. Since this hidden reality lies within our own consciousness, the physical world around us is but an illusion.

Our purpose in this world is to convert its dark mirror image into true reality itself. It's that simple. This can only be achieved by eliminating the ego, effecting the transformation within. The degree to which we achieve this transformation is the degree to which we recognize Divine consciousness and happiness as the Source of our existence.

One Electron

In true endless reality, there is, in fact, only one electron, but on our side of the mirror it appears as countless numbers of electrons. When a physicist observes an electron, he is looking in a mirror. It is the seeds of his own consciousness that he sees. Specifically, consciousness is staring at consciousness. But a physicist, using intellect, can only reach so far into true reality; he cannot cross over to the other side of the mirror without letting go of ego. Ego and the Light repel one another, so they can never connect. It's a Universal Law of our cosmos.

Two-thousand years ago, the *Zohar* said that this so-called halfway point is the very realm that gives birth to our physical reality, the crucible of the material world. When speaking of the hidden dimensions and the energy that dwells there, the *Zohar* states:

> "..*Everything is found in it in heaps, like the waves in the ocean...*"
> —*Zohar* Vol. 7: 83

The Proton Effect

On one side of the mirror there is one infinite Positive Light Consciousness; on our side of reality this is called a proton. Protons pose a challenge to particle physicists: if like particles repel, how is it that two or more protons can inhabit the nucleus of an atom? How can they remain side by side? Physics ascribe the answer to a phenomenon known as the *strong force*, which overcomes the tendency of protons to repel each other, forcing them to stay together in the nucleus.

Interestingly, when scientists tried to reduce the proton into even smaller parts, they found something astonishing: inside the proton there was almost nothing; alongside the proton was a massless particle with sticky properties, which they dubbed a gluon. Physicists tell us that the *gluon* is responsible for the force that binds protons together in the nucleus of an atom.

Once again we have the Tower of Babel Effect causing confusion. According to Kabbalah, the gluon is not a particle. The gluon is simply an Effect that arises when two particles of positive sharing consciousness exhibit the deeper reality that *like attracts like*. Namely, two protons stay together because they share the same consciousness. Whereas the electron behaves in ways that move it closer to our physical reality, the proton is closer to the consciousness reality of Light. This is why *like attracts like* overpowers *like forces repel* at the level of particle physics. Scientist agree, at least to the extent that they cannot detect anything physical in the gluon.

Receiving Consciousness and the Second Law

Science has discovered the forces that govern our world, but these forces appear to the scientific eye to be purposeless and mindless. However, once you understand the nature of the consciousness behind each force, everything starts to make perfect sense. Consciousness, by its very nature, exerts influences that we measure as independent forces because we are looking at the world from our side of the mirror, where *two* is part of the illusion.

Once you remove the concept of two, you begin to see that *force* and *consciousness* are one and the same. The only way to remove the idea of two on this side of the mirror is to remove the duality within you. The only way to do that is to eliminate the Adversary, for then you can become one with yourself. And more importantly, you will become one with the Light within you. This is when you experience the incomparable oneness of reality.

A Simple Ending

The reason we did not know any of this until now was due to the Adversary, who promoted egocentric behavior in order to create space between people and the truth. This is the cosmic game of hide and seek we joined when we came into this world.

The Paradox is that There *is* No Paradox

As we reach the end of this book we discover that, in fact, there is no Loschmidt paradox. Science just doesn't understand how the Law of Attraction changes as we shift toward the deeper reality of pure consciousness; it doesn't appreciate the *Alice in Wonderland Effect.* Physicists are observing reality from their limited perspective on only one side of the looking-glass when they peer into the subatomic realm.

How Left Becomes Right and Right Becomes Left

If you stand in front of a mirror and move your right arm up and down, the person in the mirror moves simultaneously. But in the mirror it's the *left* arm that moves; the arm on this side of the mirror is the Cause, the other is the Effect. It appears paradoxical that the one arm can give rise to its opposite. But if you understand the dynamics of the mirror effect, the paradox vanishes.

Time is unable to move forward and back because of its distance from the true timeless reality, where this is still possible. However, as you move closer to that deeper timeless reality, you begin to see such effects as reversibility, which is why Loschmidt and others found that molecules can reverse their movements. The timeless reality gave birth to our dimension that is its opposite, by virtue of our receiving consciousness and nature. When you understand why Creation took place, and why the Vessel wound up in an opposite reality, and why we need to *earn* our way back to the truth, science and Kabbalah are forever reconciled. The one thing that we need to factor into the equation is the Adversary.

In order to find God we must first find Satan, our Adversary, inside of us. If we do not, the illusion of a paradox in the quantum and macro world stays in place; as long as we remain motivated by ego and self-interest, things just don't add up. God is an absolute reality in the realm of consciousness, for the Light of the Creator is *consciousness*. However, in our world, God is not found. We need to bring God's Light and truth into this reality through our own transformation. If we don't, the belief that God does not exist becomes a self-fulfilling prophecy. Our world is a self-generating system driven by consciousness—*our* consciousness.

If we read this book and still cannot accept the existence of the Adversary, our skepticism will expand exponentially, and this book will go right over our heads. If we choose to see an electron as merely a building block of an atom, it will become one—at least for us. Our lack of consciousness will keep us from seeing beyond the particle or the wave. If, however, we resist our doubts, and we change internally, the world around us changes; then we catch more and more glimpses of true reality. It's a simple game. It always has been. But it's a game with life and death stakes; *death is just an illusion, but only if you have the insight to see it as such!*

The Ultimate Key

I will now hand you the key that my sainted teacher, Rav Brandwein, handed me so many years ago. This key has the power to unite opposites, and to remove space between Muslims, Jews, and Christians. It can remove the space between our atoms and the space between our desire for happiness and the attainment of that happiness.

I watched with my own eyes as my teacher exercised his power to unite opposites, to remove the space between Arabs and Jews, and between conservative and moderate Jews. When I first arrived in Israel I was a businessman from New York City, with no interest in anything spiritual or kabbalistic. And yet, through the power of my teacher's love and the Light that radiated from his essence, I was drawn into a world that changed the course of my entire life. My teacher used love to bridge the divide between himself and a simple Arab peasant, who was supposed to be his sworn enemy. And my teacher continues to do it today by being present as I write this final chapter, bridging the opposite worlds of our physical dimension and the unseen true reality.

The key behind our transformation and the transformation of the world is the concept of sharing, otherwise known as *Love Thy Neighbor as Thyself.* The secret of *Loving Thy Neighbor* is found within the second law of thermodynamics. For decades, science has claimed that the second law is the reason that we die and why the world of matter becomes increasingly disordered as energy and molecules spread out over space. Yet, the second law also affects the sun, the stellar body that gives us life.

Kabbalistically, the sun's primary consciousness (its essential purpose and function) is to share sunlight. From our standpoint, the sun does this unconditionally, day and night. In the case of the sharing sun, the second law actually explains the creation of life, as the sun's energy spreads out across space, becoming less and less organized but illuminating our planet in the process, causing photosynthesis and the conditions for life itself. Where, by contrast, the second law is at work under conditions driven by self-interest and receiving (the Adversary), it leads directly to chaos.

When we emulate the consciousness of the sun, when we act like the Divine consciousness of the Creator and share, we will cross through the looking-glass from this finite Universe to the infinity of true reality. Loving others is how we access true reality, and affect every atom in the Universe. That is nanotechnology. This is the blueprint to immortality. And its time is now.

I am reminded of a famous story, which takes on a whole new meaning in light of the technology presented in this book. A student once asked a great sage to teach him all the mysteries of the Bible and all the wisdom found inside the ancient biblical commentaries in the simplest way possible. The sage looked at him warmly and smiled. He replied, "Love thy neighbor as thyself. All the rest is commentary. Now go and learn."

Unfortunately, over the past 2000 years, humankind has not yet learned this lesson. By now, the reason for loving our neighbor unconditionally should be clear: it will bring this world into the world of endless Light, and by doing so it will give our neighbor the gift of immortality. This includes unending happiness, serenity, and pleasure.

This is the long-hidden secret the kabbalists handed down to a select few students over generations. Kabbalists received immortality (Kabbalah means "to receive") from their teachers and, in turn, those kabbalists handed it down to their students. The secret to immortality is the teaching and the energy inside the *Zohar*. The key to immortality is revealed in this book:

> *When we love another human being completely, when we share 100 Percent, then we automatically connect to the Light because like attracts like.*

The only force preventing a kabbalist from achieving immortality is the Adversary. The path of Kabbalah was originally designed to erase the Adversary from the consciousness of the practitioner. Once the Adversary is eradicated, the student would be able to share unconditionally. However, the Adversary penetrated the world. Hence, the opportunity to gain access to Kabbalah's secrets was never given to the world, and only a few kabbalists in each generation were able to do so. The ones who did attain this level of deathless existence are not seen among us with our five senses, though they walk among us every day. One day we will stand among them. Until that day comes, however, self-centered consciousness keeps a curtain over our eyes, preventing us from seeing complete reality.

The Reality of Immortality

Two-thousand years ago, it was calculated that if the goal of global immortality were not achieved by our present day, the *Zohar* would be revealed to the world to ensure a merciful transition into this indescribably blissful new reality. By practicing a little resistance each day, and sharing the *Zohar* with another human being, you can help us all achieve this goal. All that is required is that you admit the power you have given to your own ego. This is a recognition that the Adversary indeed exists inside of us—as does the Light of God—and therefore no one is to blame for our chaos except ourselves. This drastic shift in consciousness and the sharing of the *Zohar* is the key.

And now, as *Zohars* begin to make their way into the world in greater and greater numbers, and as we keep our egos in check, the Light of Immortality will begin to shine in small pockets, then in larger pools, then lakes, and finally in surging seas that will inundate us all in *Love Thy Neighbor* consciousness, and the force of death will flicker out of existence once and for all.

EPILOGUE

Life is a Movie

When we watch a movie, light reflects off a screen and enters our eyes. We are watching a reflection of light, not looking at that light directly. The images and the activity we see on that screen are not real. They are only an illusion, created by running together a series of individual, fixed images.

Our world works the same way. We never see direct light from the sun. Direct sunlight is invisible. We only see light after it strikes an object and reflects into our eyes. The world is our movie screen, and everyone around us is part of our movie. The projector of our movie is consciousness, for true reality is still and motionless; it is our consciousness that creates the illusion of motion.

Each of us is responsible for creating the movie that is our world. We each project a specific light frequency onto the screen of consensus reality. The world at large, and our personal world of family and friends, unfolds based on the sum total of our interactions and our states of consciousness. We can create and alter our own movie by sharing the *Zohar* and by loving unconditionally. And through our actions we can teach others how to share Light and create a better movie. When the entire world aligns its consciousness into one of sharing, the movie that is human existence will play on forever. This never-ending movie will feature only one kind of suspense and surprise: we'll wonder how the next moment could possibly be even more serene, pleasurable, magical, and joyful than the one we're living now.

This is our destiny. It is here for us at this very moment. We just have to choose it. According to Kabbalah, the suffering that mankind has endured for countless centuries ended in the kabbalistic calendar year 5760, which corresponds to the year 2000. The painful stories of heartbreak and sorrow are over. All that we need to do now is resist a little bit of ego, become accountable for our own chaos, and share the Light of the *Zohar* with others.

All the stories that were destined to be told have already played out over the course of human existence. The final story is now upon us. There is only one story left to be told and lived—a story that begins with the word *happy* and continues with the phrase *happily ever after.*

Immortality: The Inevitability of Eternal Life
By Rav Berg

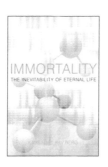

This book will totally change the way in which you perceive the world, if you simply approach its contents with an open mind and an open heart.

Most people have it backwards, dreading and battling what they see as the inevitability of aging and death. But, according to the great Kabbalist Rav Berg and the ancient wisdom of Kabbalah, it is eternal life that is inevitable.

With a radical shift in our cosmic awareness and the transformation of the collective consciousness that will follow, we can bring about the demise of the death force once and for all—in this "lifetime."

Wheels of a Soul
By Rav Berg

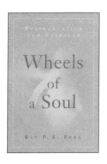

In *Wheels of a Soul*, Kabbalist Rav Berg explains why we must acknowledge and explore the lives we have already lived in order to understand the life we are living today. Make no mistake: You have been here before. Just as science is now beginning to recognize that time and space may be nothing but illusions, Rav Berg shows why death itself is the greatest illusion of all.

The Prayer of the Kabbalist: The 42 - Letter Name of God
By Yehuda Berg

According to the ancient wisdom of Kabbalah, the powerful prayer known as *Ana Bekho'ah* invokes The 42-Letter Name of God, which connects to no less than the undiluted force of creation. By tapping into this connection through the Prayer, you can leave the past behind and make a fresh start. If you recite the Prayer on a regular basis, you are able to use the force of creation to create miracles, both in your everyday life and in the world at large. This book explains the meaning behind the 42 letters and gives you practical steps for how best to connect to their power.

The Power of Kabbalah
By Yehuda Berg

Imagine your life filled with unending joy, purpose, and contentment. Imagine your days infused with pure insight and energy. This is *The Power of Kabbalah*. It is the path from the momentary pleasure that most of us settle for, to the lasting fulfillment that is yours to claim. Your deepest desires are waiting to be realized. Find out how, in this basic introduction to the ancient wisdom of Kabbalah.

God Wears Lipstick: Kabbalah for Women
By Karen Berg

For thousands of years, women were banned from studying Kabbalah, the ancient source of wisdom that explains who we are and what our purpose is in this Universe. Karen Berg changed that. She opened the doors of The Kabbalah Centre to all who would seek to learn.

In *God Wears Lipstick*, Karen Berg shares the wisdom of Kabbalah, especially as it affects you and your relationships. She reveals a woman's special place in the Universe and why women have a spiritual advantage over men. She explains how to find your soulmate and your purpose in life, and empowers you to become a better human being.

The Secret: Unlocking the Source of Joy & Fulfillment
By Michael Berg

The Secret reveals the essence of life in its most concise and powerful form. Several years before the latest "Secret" phenomenon, Michael Berg shared the amazing truths of the world's oldest spiritual wisdom in this book. In it, he has pieced together an ancient puzzle to show that our common understanding of life's purpose is actually backwards, and that anything less than complete joy and fulfillment can be changed by correcting this misperception.

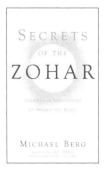

Secrets of the Zohar: Stories and Meditations to Awaken the Heart
By Michael Berg

The *Zohar*'s secrets are the secrets of the Bible, passed on as oral tradition and then recorded as a sacred text that remained hidden for thousands of years. They have never been revealed quite as they are here in these pages, which decipher the codes behind the best stories of the ancient sages and offer a special meditation for each one. Entire portions of the *Zohar* are presented, with the Aramaic and its English translation in side-by-side columns. This allows you to scan and to read aloud so that you can draw on the *Zohar*'s full energy and achieve spiritual transformation. Open this book and open your heart to the Light of the *Zohar*!

Living Kabbalah: A Practical System for Making the Power Work for You
By Yehuda Berg

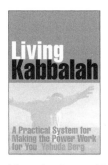

Living Kabbalah is a unique system of technology meant for you to use to transform your life and achieve true and lasting fulfillment. In these pages, you will find practical tools and exercises to help you break negative patterns, overcome challenges, and incorporate the time-tested wisdom of Kabbalah into your daily life. Noted author and teacher Yehuda Berg provides a clear blueprint that guides you step-by-step along the path toward the ultimate attainment of all that you need and desire.

Tap into a greater power—the power of Kabbalah—and learn to live more fully, richly, and joyfully every day, starting today!

NANO TECHNOLOGY OF MIND OVER MATTER

The Living Kabbalah System™: Levels 1 & 2

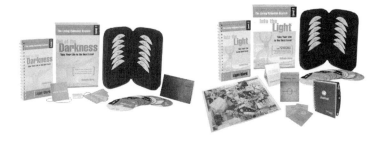

Take Your Life to the Next Level™ with this step-by-step, 23-day system for transforming your life and achieving lasting fulfillment.

Created by Yehuda Berg and based on his belief that Kabbalah should be lived, not merely studied, this revolutionary interactive system incorporates the latest learning strategies, addressing all three learning styles:

- Auditory (recorded audio sessions)

- Visual (workbook with written concepts and graphics)

- Tactile (written exercises, self-assessments, and physical tools)

The sturdy carrying case makes the system easy and convenient to use, in the car, at the gym, on a plane, wherever and whenever you choose. Learn from today's great Kabbalah leaders in an intimate, one-on-one learning atmosphere. You get practical, actionable tools and exercises to integrate the wisdom of Kabbalah into your daily life. In just 23 days you can learn to live with greater intensity, be more successful in business and relationships, and achieve your dreams. Why wait? Take your life to the next level starting today.

THE ZOHAR

Composed more than 2,000 years ago, the *Zohar* is a set of 23 books, a commentary on biblical and spiritual matters in the form of conversations among spiritual masters. But to describe the *Zohar* only in physical terms is greatly misleading. In truth, the *Zohar* is nothing less than a powerful tool for achieving the most important purposes of our lives. It was given to all humankind by the Creator to bring us protection, to connect us with the Creator's Light, and ultimately to fulfill our birthright of true spiritual transformation.

More than eighty years ago, when The Kabbalah Centre was founded, the *Zohar* had virtually disappeared from the world. Few people in the general population had ever heard of it. Whoever sought to read it—in any country, in any language, at any price—faced a long and futile search.

Today all this has changed. Through the work of The Kabbalah Centre and the editorial efforts of Michael Berg, the *Zohar* is now being brought to the world, not only in the original Aramaic language but also in English. The new English *Zohar* provides everything for connecting to this sacred text on all levels: the original Aramaic text for scanning; an English translation; and clear, concise commentary for study and learning.

THE KABBALAH CENTRE®

What is Kabbalah?

Kabbalah is the world's oldest body of spiritual wisdom, containing the long-hidden keys to the secrets of the Universe, as well as the keys to the mysteries of the human heart and soul. It's a workable system that allows you to understand your purpose for being here experiencing the joy you were put on Earth to have. In fact, that's what Kabbalah means to receive, to get.

Kabbalah teaches that in order to claim the gifts you were created to receive, you need to earn them by undertaking your spiritual work the process of fundamentally transforming yourself as you climb out of the darkness and into the Light. By helping you recognize the sources of negativity in your own mind and heart, Kabbalah gives you the tools for positive change.

Kabbalistic teachings explain the complexities of the material and the nonmaterial Universe and the physical and metaphysical nature of all humankind.

Moses, Pythagoras, and Sir Isaac Newton are a few of the individuals who studied Kabbalah to understand the spiritual laws of the Universe and their effect on the physical world.

Kabbalah is meant to be used, not merely learned. It can help you remove chaos, pain, and suffering from your life and bring you clarity, understanding, and freedom.

Who Can Study?

Today, millions of people of all faiths have discovered the wisdom and experienced the powerful effects of studying Kabbalah.

Why shouldn't they? Kabbalah works. When the wisdom and practical tools of Kabbalah are applied in life, positive experiences are the result. And Kabbalah can enhance the practice of any religion.

What Is The Kabbalah Centre®?

The Kabbalah Centre® is a spiritual and educational organization dedicated to bringing the wisdom of Kabbalah to the world. The Centre itself has existed for more than 80 years, but its spiritual lineage extends back to Rav Isaac Luria in the 16th century and even further back to Rav Shimon bar Yochai, who revealed the principal text of Kabbalah, the *Zohar*, more than 2,000 years ago.

The Kabbalah Centre® was founded in 1922 by Rav Yehuda Ashlag, one of the greatest kabbalists of the 20th Century. When Rav Ashlag left this world, leadership of The Centre was taken on by Rav Yehuda Brandwein. Before his passing, Rav Brandwein designated Rav Berg as director of The Kabbalah Centre®. Now, for more than 30 years, The Centre has been under the direction of Rav Berg, his wife Karen Berg, and their sons, Yehuda Berg and Michael Berg.

Although there are many scholarly studies of Kabbalah, The Kabbalah Centre® does not teach Kabbalah as an academic discipline but as a way of creating a better life. The mission of The Kabbalah Centre® is to make the practical tools and spiritual teachings of Kabbalah available and accessible to everyone regardless of religion, ethnicity, gender, or age.

The Kabbalah Centre® makes no promises. But if people are willing to work hard to grow and become actively sharing, caring, and tolerant human beings, Kabbalah teaches that they will then experience fulfillment and joy in a way previously unknown to them. This sense of fulfillment, however, comes gradually and is always the result of the student's spiritual work.

Our ultimate goal is for all humanity to gain the happiness and ful-fillment that is our true destiny.

Kabbalah teaches its students to question and test everything they learn. One of the most important teachings of Kabbalah is that there is no coercion in spirituality.

What Does The Kabbalah Centre® Offer?

Local Kabbalah Centres around the world offer onsite lectures, classes, study groups, holiday celebrations, and a community of teachers and fellow students. To find a Centre near you, go to www.kabbalah.com.

For those of you unable to access a physical Kabbalah Centre due to the constraints of location or time, we have other ways to par-ticipate in The Kabbalah Centre® community.

At www.kabbalah.com, we feature online blogs, newsletters, weekly wisdom, a store, and much more.

It's a wonderful way to stay tuned in and in touch, and it gives you access to programs that will expand your mind and challenge you to continue your spiritual work.

Student Support

The Kabbalah Centre® empowers people to take responsibility for their own lives. It's about the teachings, not the teachers. But on your journey to personal growth, things can be unclear and some-times rocky, so it is helpful to have a coach or teacher.

All Student Support instructors have studied Kabbalah under the direct supervision of Kabbalist Rav Berg, widely recognized as the preeminent kabbalist of our time.

We have also created opportunities for you to interact with other Student Support students through study groups, monthly connections, holiday retreats, and other events held around the country.

Our wish is that everyone who discovers the wisdom
within these pages

will take action to transform both their lives
and the entire world.

Eternal love and thanks to the Rav and Karen, Yehuda
and Michael, their families and the Chevre.

Betsy, Charlie and Elijah Ray Davis